PATTERN
AND DESIGN WITH
DYNAMIC SYMMETRY

EDWARD B. EDWARDS

PATTERN
AND DESIGN WITH
DYNAMIC SYMMETRY

HOW TO
CREATE ART DECO
GEOMETRICAL DESIGNS

DOVER PUBLICATIONS, INC., NEW YORK

This Dover edition, first published in 1967, is an unabridged republication of the work originally published by The Century Company in 1932 under the title *Dynamarhythmic Design*.

Standard Book Number: 486-21756-6
Library of Congress Catalog Card Number: 66-30211

Manufactured in the United States of America
Dover Publications, Inc.
180 Varick Street
New York, N. Y. 10014

TO

WILFORD S. CONROW

AND

FRANCIS L. NOBLE

TWO FRIENDS
TO WHOM THE AUTHOR
IS GRATEFUL
FOR
THEIR INTEREST
AND
ENCOURAGEMENT

FOREWORD

In the autumn of 1917, Jay Hambidge was giving a series of talks on Dynamic Symmetry to a small group of students, including Wilford S. Conrow, Chester Beach, Miss Frances Morris, Miss Eugenie Shonnard, Miss Christine Herter, Louis P. Skidmore, Sergent Kendall, George H. Whittle, in the office of George H. Whittle at 70 Fifth Avenue, New York. Mr. Whittle had formerly been assistant art director of the *Century Magazine* and was deeply sympathetic with all matters pertaining to art. Shortly after these talks had started, Mr. Whittle extended an invitation to the author, who was glad to avail himself of the opportunity to attend these meetings. He had long been dissatisfied with the arts of design as they then existed in this and other countries and was constantly searching for a principle which would admit of the building up of a new design fabric on a logical foundation. During his first talk with Mr. Hambidge he was convinced that Mr. Hambidge had found such a principle, and that night the author worked till very late experimenting with the root rectangles. The possibilities from the standpoint of pattern alone seemed to be endless, and he was very much excited over the matter. His first experiment consisted in crossing the root rectangles and their principal structural lines, at right angles, as in Fig. 1, with alternate areas in black and white.

The resultant tile patterns were very pleasing, and as far as the author was aware, were entirely new. In order to facilitate the drawing of the root and 1.618 rectangles the author cut several triangles from heavy bristol board. The root-three triangle was already at hand in the common 30 and 60 degree instrument. Shortly after that he commenced to experiment with the spiral forms within the rectangles, drawing the spirals by the method of construction which Mr. Hambidge

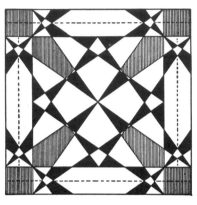

FIG. 1

had taught his students. A small Greek bronze ornament in the author's collection was very suggestive, and resulted in a number of more or less successful designs. A drawing of this bronze is shown herewith, actual size, Fig. 2. The author shortly thereafter found that there is only one mathematical curve which will fulfill the conditions of this design, and that is the logarithmic spiral which completely fills a rectangle, and which permits of the spiral being reversed with a side of the rectangle as an axis, without a break in the curve. As the author's mathematical knowledge was insufficient to determine the exact ratio of this rectangle, he submitted the question to his friend Professor H. B. Mitchell, at that time instructor in mathematics at Columbia University, New York, who was kind enough to solve the problem for him. The ratio of the rectangle is 1 to 1.5388. Some-time thereafter the author found from a study of the examples of early Mycenaean and Cretan art in the Metropolitan Museum of Art, that these reversed spiral forms were already in use, in a free way, 1600 years B.C. As the Mycenaeans and Cretans used

FIG. 2

natural shell forms to a great extent in their decoration, there seems to be no doubt as to the origin of the spiral forms they used.[1]

[1] *The Palace of Minos at Knossos,* by Sir Arthur Evans (London, The Macmillan Company, Ltd., 1921-1930).
Mykene, by H. Schliemann (Leipzig, 1878).

Mr. Hambidge, while fully aware of the importance of the principles he was teaching, from the standpoint of the architect, the sculptor and the painter, was not aware at this time of their importance from the standpoint of the designer of ornament, and was consequently amazed when he was shown the result of the author's experiments. This was not strange as Mr. Hambidge was primarily an illustrator, and had had no training in design in its more restricted sense. He was, moreover, burdened with the necessity of proving his theories to the world of art, and was so fully occupied with teaching his conclusions and with the analysis of Egyptian and Greek design that he had, for the time being at least, no time for creative effort.

The author had no doubt, as far as he himself was concerned, that the Egyptians and the Greeks used the system of symmetry which Mr. Hambidge had rediscovered, and perceived immediately the possibility of building up a new structural fabric in design, based on the geometrical principles of order and proportion inherent in the system. Personal investigations, and analysis of objects in the author's collection convinced him very early in his association with Mr. Hambidge that the latter's theories were primarily true. On the other hand, the author could not agree with the assertion of Mr. Hambidge that the art was lost before the Roman period, because of two red Samian vases in the author's collection which conform to the system, as well as several Sidonian glass cups. Some time later, The Great Chalice of Antioch, which is of the first century A.D., was also analyzed by the author and the result was published in Dr. Gustavus A. Eisen's great monograph on the chalice.[2]

The quarters of Mr. Whittle were quite restricted, and such was the

---

[2] *The Great Chalice of Antioch*, by Gustavus A. Eisen (privately printed for Kouchakji Frères, New York, 1923), p. 184.

author's interest in the matter that he offered Mr. Hambidge the use of his studio, at that time located at 50 West 12th St., New York, and also volunteered to organize a class of artists if Mr. Hambidge would consent to lecture to them. Mr. Hambidge was quite enthusiastic, and shortly thereafter the lectures began to a group of the author's friends, including Wilford S. Conrow, Howard Giles, Frederick D. Hull, Rev. George D. Graeff, Albert Southwick, W. Gedney Beatty, A. L. Barney, Rutherford Boyd, Mr. and Mrs. Troy Kinney, John Scott Williams, the author's son, Albert, and others. The news of the lectures spread rapidly, and the class was soon filled with a large group of enthusiastic students, most of whom were men of recognized ability in the art world, and included such names as Robert Henri, George Bellows, Leon Kroll, Jonas Lie, Alfred Maurer, Welles Bosworth, the architect, Fahim Kouchakji, Gustavus A. Eisen, the archeologist, and many others.

About this time the author was engaged on some drawings for the Classical Department of the Metropolitan Museum of Art, and took advantage of the opportunity to talk concerning the subject of Mr. Hambidge's theories to Miss Gisela A. Richter, who at that time was the assistant curator of the department under Dr. Edward Robinson. Miss Richter became very much interested and made an appointment to meet Mr. Hambidge and the author at the museum. The author also talked to Mr. Henry W. Kent, secretary of the museum, and as a result a meeting was arranged, where, in the board room of the museum, Mr. Hambidge addressed a group of the museum's staff and several invited guests. In preparation for this talk, Mr. Hambidge made an analysis of several vases and kylikes of the museum collection. This was the beginning of his exhaustive study of the subject and led to the publication of his book, *Dynamic Symmetry, The Greek Vase*, by the Yale University Press in 1920.

Mr. Rutherford Boyd, who was among the first to attend the lectures in the author's studio, and with whom the author had been rather closely associated while Mr. Boyd was assistant art director of the *Ladies Home Journal*, and later art director of the *Delineator*, was much interested in the possibilities of Mr. Hambidge's ideas and joined the author in his investigations. Mr. Hambidge, Mr. Boyd, and the author talked of an association for the purpose of the practical application of Dynamic Design to modern needs in all fields of design and manufacture, and also for the purpose of teaching the principles, and for the publication of books on the subject. Mr. Hambidge wrote the prospectus, but the idea of the association failed of realization, because Mr. Hambidge shortly thereafter became occupied with his lectures at Yale and Harvard Universities and with the publication of *The Diagonal* by the Yale University Press.

The lectures in the author's studio continued throughout the Spring of 1918, and were discontinued only because the quarters were not large enough to accommodate the increasing number of students. Through his old friend, Mr. Horace Moran, at that time chairman of the current work committee of the Architectural League of New York, the author obtained permission for Mr. Hambidge to use the League rooms, where he delivered a series of ten lectures to a large group of students early in 1919.

Mr. Boyd and the author continued to work on the designs, but were greatly handicapped because the free hand curves were not sufficiently accurate for the work, and no instruments for the drawing of these curves were manufactured. In order to obviate this difficulty, Mr. Boyd constructed some curves and cut them out of bristol board and later from celluloid. Some time later the author had an instrument made similar to that invented by Francis C. Penrose, and described by Mr. Hambidge on page 57 of his book on the Parthenon.[3] This instrument, which Mr. Penrose called a helicograph, while theoretically correct in principle, was cumbersome, and therefore was discarded by the author in favor of the celluloid curves.

Mr. Boyd published the result of his own and the author's investigations in *Architecture* in August, 1929, illustrated by his own drawings.[4]

[3] *The Parthenon and Other Greek Temples: Their Dynamic Symmetry*, by Jay Hambidge (New Haven, Yale University Press, 1924).

[4] At the time the above was written the author was not aware that a second article by Mr. Boyd appeared in the April, 1930, issue of *Architecture*.

CONTENTS

ILLUSTRATIONS

INTRODUCTION

This book has been written to show how the principles of dynamic symmetry may be applied to the designing of pattern. The name *Dynamarhythmic Design* has been coined advisedly by the writer to distinguish the subject from the term *Dynamic Symmetry*, used by Mr. Hambidge, and applying to dynamic design in its broader sense. Mr. Hambidge has written a great deal about the analysis of rectangular areas, but much work remains to be done before a full understanding of this subject may be had from the standpoint of the artist.

The author, in an effort to make this an impersonal matter, has attempted to confine himself in these designs, with a few exceptions, to an enunciation and employment of the principles underlying dynamic design, feeling that these principles are of infinitely more importance than any individual conceptions. The designs should be regarded as purely structural; consequently the results could be achieved independently by any number of trained craftsmen having an equal knowledge of the design principles involved. It is in the individual treatment and amplification of the designs, and their application to various uses, that the craftsman may show his artistic ability and individuality.

Without desiring to appear unduly modest, the author confesses that he is still a student of the subject. So many problems remain to be solved, that it was only with the greatest reluctance, and after repeated urging by his friends, that he decided to publish a book at this time. For example, there is much to be done with combinations of rectangles and their individual spirals. In experimenting with the designs the author has found, in order to fulfill certain preconceived ideas, that a combination of two or more different spirals was necessary.

Many students of dynamic symmetry complain that it is too complicated for the average student to grasp; for this reason a number of designs of comparatively elementary character have been shown, leading up to the more complicated patterns by graded steps. The author feels that the principles are quite easily understood; the shapes of the root and the 1.618 rectangles may be arrived at by the most simple constructions; in fact all of the designs contained in this book have been made without the use of figures, which have been used merely to define ratios of end to side of the rectangles, which could not be otherwise, or with difficulty, identified.

It is essential for the student to become thoroughly familiar with the principles of Dynamarhythmic Design; to this end constant drawing and redrawing of the rectangles is advisable, as it is only in this way that he can learn to think in its terms. The student should also keep a record of the structure of the less obvious designs he may make, as it is sometimes difficult, in retrospect, to remember the method used in their planning. The construction of a design may be simple, while on the contrary an analysis of it may be comparatively difficult.

The construction of the spiral curves is the most difficult problem with which the student has to contend; for that reason all of the spirals used in the designs are shown, actual size, and have only to be carefully traced and cut from stiff bristol board or sheet celluloid. In the printed plates the only danger may be in distortion caused by shrinkage in the process of photo-engraving, or in a like shrinkage of the paper. On the whole it would be much more satisfactory for the student to plot his own curves. How to do this will be fully explained in a separate chapter.

Most students struggle to acquire a knowledge of a mass of details which bear no relationship to one another, nor to any general conception. In Dynamarhythmic Design, not only are the forms related harmoniously, but the areas are related as well. Within these areas the artist may use such forms, natural or otherwise, as his caprice or fancy may dictate, providing that he keep in mind the proportional relationships which belong naturally within the parent form, or, in other words, that he relate the parts consistently to the whole. It may be argued that design may become an intellectual process, but it is just as important for the designer to understand the laws of harmoniously related forms and areas, as it is for the musical composer to be familiar with the laws of harmony and counterpoint.

A design arouses a visual emotion. If it is a good design the emotion is a pleasant one, and vice versa. If there are laws of harmony and proportion which can be learned and applied in the planning of our work, it is foolish to argue that these laws should not be used because they do not allow us sufficient scope for the free employment of our innate artistic ability. Great art is impersonal, and the great artist will willingly accept the limits imposed by a logical use of known essential principles. Where great art is produced, whether in painting, sculpture, architecture or design, or in music, it is the result of the use of the fundamental laws of nature, which underlie the structure and purpose of our being and to which we react, consciously or unconsciously. It is the superior sensitiveness to, and perhaps knowledge of these laws, whether they be of rhythm, form, proportion, or color, or of sound, which distinguishes the artist.

From the earliest times the artist has been searching for coördinating principles, which would bring order out of chaos. In contending, in our day, with modern problems of architectural design, we cannot start with an ideal condition, unless it be in the case of a monument or a similar structure which stands entirely alone, and is therefore uncontaminated by the close proximity of other structures of an inharmonious character. An ideal condition can be conceived of, where an entire city might be the conception of some super-architect, working with the coöperation of the sculptor and the painter, to the end that all of the buildings and their decorations may be related to some general thematic plan. But the millennium will not arrive in our day, and man will not become really civilized until he learns to subordinate his individual needs and desires to the general good of his fellows.

It is inevitable in a book of this character, especially as the author is not a mathematician, and has had practically no experience in writing, that many errors of statement may have been made; for these he apologizes. In his past experience, he has arrived at many conclusions which he was forced on further investigation, and after more considered judgment, to abandon. The truth is often self-evident, but it is more often elusive.

PATTERN AND DESIGN WITH DYNAMIC SYMMETRY

CHAPTER I

GENERAL THEORY

As the circle is said to be a special case of the ellipse, so the square may be said to be a special case of the rectangle. In Greek and Egyptian design it was considered to be the unit of area, and so we shall consider it for purposes of Dynamarhythmic Design. The square is the static point, or, we may say, the point of balance. It is fixed. From

<-------- *Decreasing to Infinity*   *Unity*   *Increasing to Infinity* -------->

FIG. I

it on the one side we have rectangles gradually increasing in length to infinity, and on the other side gradually decreasing, likewise to infinity, Fig. 1. The rectangles to the left of the unit square are all reciprocals of corresponding rectangles to the right of the unit square. The artist, however, is concerned only with the rectangles which come within the practical range of his work.

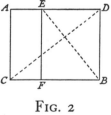

FIG. 2

These rectangles, when properly subdivided, are dynamic; they have the quality of form in motion. To introduce into a rectangle the dynamic quality, or the quality of form in motion, we first draw a rectangle AB, Fig. 2, and then draw a diagonal CD. From B we erect BE perpendicular to the diagonal CD, which cuts from the parent rectangle AB, the area FD. This area is the same shape as AB, but is at right angles to it. It is the reciprocal of AB.

3

The reciprocal of any rectangle may be found by dividing the length of its side into its end; for example, in a root-two rectangle, the ratio of end to side is 1.000 to 1.4142; 1.000 divided by 1.4142 equals .7071. The reciprocal is therefore in the ratio of .7071 to 1.000 or one half the area of the root-two rectangle. In Fig. 2, if the length FB is divided into BD, it gives the same ratio as BD divided into BC. This principle applies to rectangles of any length. Fig. 3 will illustrate this.

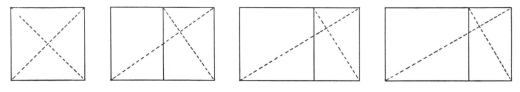

FIG. 3

We first have the unit square (which has no reciprocal, as its crossed diagonals completely fill the space), and a series of rectangles gradually increasing in length, with the diagonals drawn in each as shown in Fig. 2. Observe that each rectangle has its own reciprocal. As the rectangle increases in length, the reciprocal decreases in width. Referring again to Fig. 3, we come to a consideration of the area which remains after the reciprocal has been subtracted from a rectangle. This area was called a *gnomon* by the Greeks, and was defined by Aristotle as that shape which when added to any other shape whatsoever, left the resultant figure unchanged except in area. In Fig. 4A, let AB be any rectangle, and BC its reciprocal; the remaining figure, AD, is the gnomon of AB. In Fig. 4B, we

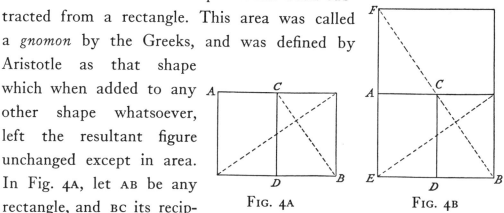

FIG. 4A   FIG. 4B

add a gnomon to the rectangle AB by producing the end of the rectangle EA and the diagonal BC, till they meet in F. By completing the rectangle FB, we have increased its size but left its shape unchanged, and we can continue the process indefinitely. This illustrates the property of continued similarity of form increasing in a continued ratio to infinity. It is the principle of growth, and is the basis of Dynama-rhythmic Design. In Fig. 5 the reverse of the process is shown: Let AB be

any rectangle; draw the diagonals CD and BE, and the line EF, cutting off the reciprocal FD and the gnomon AF: draw GH, IJ, KL, etc., in each case from the point where the diagonals of the rectangles cross the lines cutting off the recip-rocals; and we have the gnomons revolving

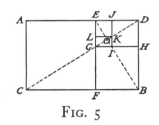

FIG. 5

around the pole o at the intersection of the two diagonals, and decreas-ing in a constant ratio to infinity. This is true of any rectangle as may be seen from Fig. 6 in which the gnomons are numbered 1, 2, 3,

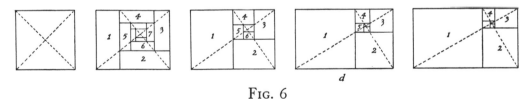

FIG. 6

4, 5, 6, etc.; a special case of this series is the rectangle of the whirling squares, Fig. 6d, so called by Mr. Hambidge, in which the gnomons are squares, and the ratio 1.000 to 1.618. Following the lead of Mr. Ham-bidge, the author has called this series *the rectan-gles of the whirling gnomons.* A gnomon may also be in the shape of a carpenter's square, Fig. 7. Any rectangle may be increased or decreased in size in this way without change of shape, by

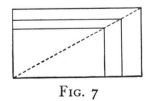

FIG. 7

the addition or subtraction of similar gnomons, and this may be done, but not necessarily, in a constant ratio of end to side of the rectangle. This principle is known to all artists and draftsmen. In the spiral of the shell, or in the logarithmic spiral, the gnomon may be any incre-ment of growth, however small; but for design purposes, we shall in

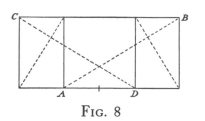

Fig. 8

most instances consider a gnomon as the area bounded by any two radii vectors at right angles to each other, and a segment of the spiral.

Let us consider further interesting sub-divisions of the rectangle. Take for ex-ample Fig. 6d, which is a whirling square rectangle, and add a recip-rocal to the other end as in Fig. 8. We now have a compound figure composed of two whirling square rectangles AB and CD overlapping to the extent of a square, which is the gnomon of either and common to both. This compound figure is a root-five rectangle, (1.618 + .618 = 2.236, the square root of 5). If we take a figure

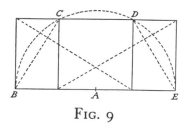

Fig. 9

similar to Fig. 8, (Fig. 9), and bisect the gnomon at A and describe a semicircle BCDE, with AB as radius, it will cut the side of the rectangle

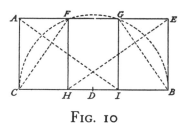

Fig. 10

at C and D, defining the points where the lines cutting off the reciprocals of the 1.618 rectangles are drawn. Any rectangle greater than root-four, or two squares, may be similarly and directly subdivided:—Take any rectangle AB greater than the root-four, Fig. 10, and bisect the side CB at D; with DC as radius describe the semi-circle CFGB intersecting the side AE of the rectangle at the points F and G. Draw FH and GI cutting off the reciprocals. This method of subdivi-

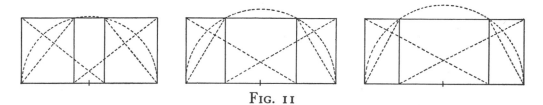

FIG. 11

sion, which is continuous, is shown in Fig. 11. By subdividing a rectangle in this way we are, primarily, cutting it into two rectangles, alike in shape, but unlike in size; viz. a rectangle plus its reciprocal, Fig. 12,

so that the entire rectangle is a compound figure. A further development of these principles of subdivision is shown in Figs. 13A and B. We commence with a rectangle AB, composed of two whirling square rectangles overlapping to

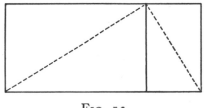

FIG. 12

the extent of a square (root-five), and by extending the diagonals of the reciprocals of the 1.618 rectangles until they meet the extended

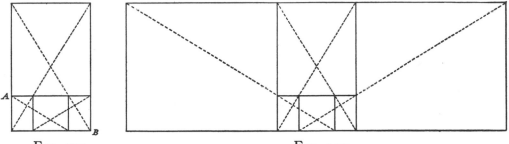

FIG. 13A   FIG. 13B

ends of the root-five rectangle we produce a rectangle of a similar shape to the reciprocal. In Fig. 13B, we extend the diagonals laterally and have still further subdivisions. But as it is the desire of the author to confine himself to the elementary principles of Dynamarhythmic Design, we shall leave further speculative investigations to the mathematically inclined student.

The foregoing series of rectangles, in which the property of continued proportion and of similarity of shape are inherent, all have potential dynamic qualities and give a great number of structural skeleton forms which are of great practical use in composition or design; they belong to an infinite series of which the root and the 1.618 are the regular rectangles, for the reason that in the 1.618 rectangle the gnomons are squares to infinity, and in the root rectangles, the area of the square on the side is an even multiple of the area of the square on the end, and the reciprocals are even divisions of the rectangles, which may in addition be divided and subdivided into terms of similar rectangles to infinity, without a remainder. While the root and the 1.618 or regular rectangles are more fascinating in their remarkable coincidences of forms, and in the case of the root-rectangles may be evenly divided in terms of their reciprocals, the principles of divisibility into gnomonic forms in a continued ratio apply as well to the "irregular" or "in-between" rectangles, which can be described individually only in terms of the ratio of the end to the side. A scale of the ratios of end to side may be drawn within any rectangle, giving the harmonious linear relationships which properly belong within that rectangle. Fig. 14.

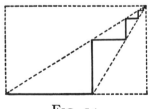

FIG. 14

While the Egyptians and the Greeks may not have used these irregular rectangles, the author feels that there is a great opportunity for modern investigation in this field, and that the sum and substance of dynamic symmetry rests on the principles of continued proportion and of divisibility into similar shapes which are inherent in any rectangle. This idea is at variance with the conclusions of Mr. Hambidge, who contended that the root-rectangles and the 1.618 rectangle and its derivatives alone enter into the dynamic system. He was even in doubt as to whether the root-two and the root-three rectangles should be included. In No. 9, page 182 of *The Diagonal*[1] he says:—

" . . . Its use, (root-two), however is limited, and as has been mentioned in *The Diagonal*, probably constitutes, with the root-three rectangle, an intermediate type of symmetry between the static and the dynamic. If this be true then the dynamic is the class made by the root-five area as the parent shape, and its logical derivatives. Or perhaps we have in root-two and root-three a minor dynamic class. At any rate the root-two rectangle was the shape first adopted by the Greeks when they changed from a linear to an area system of measurement for design purposes, or a system based upon the relationship of a side to a diagonal of a square."

In the author's opinion, Mr. Hambidge's greatest contribution to the theory of design was in the placing of two diagonals in a rectangle, the one crossing the other from the opposite end at right angles and thereby cutting off the reciprocal to the rectangle and defining the law of continued proportion of end to side within the limits of the space. The writer feels that the beauty of nature does not depend on any one combination or series of combinations of ratios, but on the principle of continued proportional growth and on similarity of form. The spirals of shells do not conform to one, but to many rectangular ratios, and the same thing holds true of the growth of plants. The author, however, has no desire to confuse the issue by a fruitless discussion of nature's processes of plant and animal growth, (the student interested in these subjects may consult the books of Church,[2] Cook,[3] Colman[4] and Thompson[5]), but is concerned mainly with the effort to generalize and to consolidate the principles of growth into a theory that may be readily understood by the artist and designer, and utilized in the practice of his daily work.

[1] *The Diagonal* (New Haven, Conn., Yale University Press, July, 1920).   [2] *Relation of Phyllotaxis to Mechanical Laws* (Oxford, 1901, 1903).   [3] *The Curves of Life* (New York, Henry Holt and Company, 1914).   [4] *Nature's Harmonic Unity* (New York, G. P. Putnam's Sons, 1912).   [5] *Growth and Form* (Cambridge: at the University Press, 1917).

CHAPTER II

GENERAL CONSTRUCTION OF ROOT AND RELATED RECTANGLES

The root rectangles, as previously mentioned, are those in which the area of the square on the side is an even multiple of the square on the end, and are all evenly divisible in terms of their reciprocals (viz: root-two, two reciprocals, root-three, three reciprocals, etc.). The author's method of drawing the root rectangles is shown herewith, Fig. 1, and thereby any root rectangle may be produced directly and with great accuracy. To the side AB of the unit square AC, add one half the length of AB, or .500, which gives us the point D. With D as a center, and DA as a radius, describe the arc AE, intersecting the extended base line of the unit square, which is common to all the root rectangles in the diagram; E defines the length BE of the root-two rectangle, 1.4142. Each successive root rectangle may be produced by the simple addition of .500 to the radius of the preceding rectangle. Therefore the radius of root-two is 1.500, root-three 2.000, root-

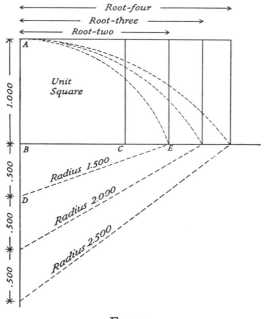

FIG. 1

four 2.500, root-five 3.000, etc., to infinity. In each case, the diagonal of the preceding rectangle becomes the base line of the succeeding rectangle.

Another interesting series of rectangles may be obtained by the above method of construction by adding to the side AB of the unit square other fractional parts. A table is given on page 12, showing the resultant rectangles obtained.

All of these rectangles, which may be extended to infinity, are capable of dynamic subdivision, not only in terms of their gnomons whirling around the pole, but in terms of themselves, and of their reciprocals. With the exception of the root-rectangles, which form part of the complete series, their possibilities have not been fully investigated by the author, but they are recorded here for the benefit of those who may be interested in experimenting with them. The field is as yet unexplored, as they are new additions to the theory of Dynamic Design. How they can be used is the problem for the modern designer to solve, just as the Greeks and the Egyptians solved their problems of design in their own way, and created their masterpieces with the knowledge at their disposal.

The construction of these rectangles is simply an application of the method of obtaining a mean proportional as shown in Prop. 13, Book

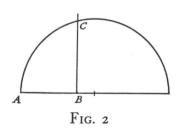

FIG. 2

VI of Euclid, Fig. 2. In the diagram, AB represents the unit end of the rectangles and the lengths of the sides are measured on the line BC extended, perpendicular to AB. In each instance the side of the rectangle is the mean proportional between 1.000 or the unit end, and double the radius minus 1.000, or the square root of double the radius minus 1.000.

Radius $1\frac{1}{4}$,   Reciprocal $\frac{2}{3}$ of Rectangle

″	$1\frac{1}{2}$,	″	$\frac{2}{4}=\frac{1}{2}$	″	″	$=$ root-two
″	$1\frac{3}{4}$,	″	$\frac{2}{5}$	″	″	
″	2,	″	$\frac{2}{6}=\frac{1}{3}$	″	″	$=$ root-three
″	$2\frac{1}{4}$,	″	$\frac{2}{7}$	″	″	
″	$2\frac{1}{2}$,	″	$\frac{2}{8}=\frac{1}{4}$	″	″	$=$ root-four

Radius $1\frac{1}{6}$,   Reciprocal $\frac{3}{4}$ of Rectangle

″	$1\frac{2}{6}$,	″	$\frac{3}{5}$	″	″	
″	$1\frac{3}{6}$,	″	$\frac{3}{6}=\frac{1}{2}$	″	″	$=$ root-two
″	$1\frac{4}{6}$,	″	$\frac{3}{7}$	″	″	
″	$1\frac{5}{6}$,	″	$\frac{3}{8}$	″	″	
″	2,	″	$\frac{3}{9}=\frac{1}{3}$	″	″	$=$ root-three

Radius $1\frac{1}{8}$,   Reciprocal $\frac{4}{5}$ of Rectangle

″	$1\frac{2}{8}$,	″	$\frac{4}{6}=\frac{2}{3}$	″	″	
″	$1\frac{3}{8}$,	″	$\frac{4}{7}$	″	″	
″	$1\frac{4}{8}$,	″	$\frac{4}{8}=\frac{1}{2}$	″	″	$=$ root-two
″	$1\frac{5}{8}$,	″	$\frac{4}{9}$	″	″	
″	$1\frac{6}{8}$,	″	$\frac{4}{10}=\frac{2}{5}$	″	″	
″	$1\frac{7}{8}$,	″	$\frac{4}{11}$	″	″	
″	2,	″	$\frac{4}{12}=\frac{1}{3}$	″	″	$=$ root-three

Radius $1\frac{1}{10}$,   Reciprocal $\frac{5}{6}$ of Rectangle

″	$1\frac{2}{10}$,	″	$\frac{5}{7}$	″	″	
″	$1\frac{3}{10}$,	″	$\frac{5}{8}$	″	″	
″	$1\frac{4}{10}$,	″	$\frac{5}{9}$	″	″	
″	$1\frac{5}{10}$,	″	$\frac{5}{10}=\frac{1}{2}$	″	″	$=$ root-two
″	$1\frac{6}{10}$,	″	$\frac{5}{11}$	″	″	
″	$1\frac{7}{10}$,	″	$\frac{5}{12}$	″	″	
″	$1\frac{8}{10}$,	″	$\frac{5}{13}$	″	″	
″	$1\frac{9}{10}$,	″	$\frac{5}{14}$	″	″	
″	2,	″	$\frac{5}{15}=\frac{1}{3}$	″	″	$=$ root-three

CHAPTER III

HOW TO CONSTRUCT A LOGARITHMIC SPIRAL

When the Greeks discovered how to obtain a mean proportional between two lines (Euclid, Book VI, Prop. 13), they discovered how to construct a logarithmic spiral, but as far as we know, they failed to apply their knowledge to that end, and it was not until 1638 that René Descartes, the French mathematician, in letters to Mersenne, described the method of its construction.

The spirals of the Ionic volutes are merely approximations of true logarithmic spirals, and were drawn with a compass by means of successive quadrant arcs; the actual compass marks have been found on fragments of Ionic capitals. The well-known method here shown, Fig. 1, is re-drawn from *Die Architectur*, by Professor Buhlmann. The quadrant arcs are indicated by Roman numerals, and the centers of the arcs are indicated by corresponding numerals in the eye of the volute (shown enlarged). A curve constructed by this method would be useless how-

ever, for drawing Dynama-rhythmic designs, because any two closely contiguous curves, if drawn from the same pole, would not follow each other smoothly.

Descartes discovered that if B and c are two points on the curve Fig. 2, its length from o to B is to the radius

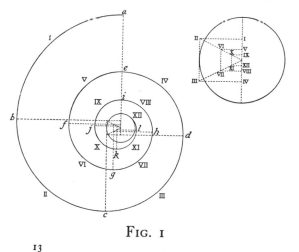

FIG. 1

vector OB, as the length of the curve from o to c, is to the radius vector OC. The curve cuts the radii vectors at a constant angle. The

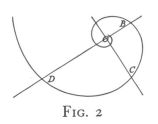

FIG. 2

angle BCO is equal to CDO, etc., and the segments of the curve defined by the radii vectors are in a continued ratio. Each successive segment of the figure bounded by the curve, and any two radii vectors, is a gnomon of the preceding shape and increases likewise in a continued ratio. Any radius vector which bisects the angle made by any two radii vectors is a mean proportional between them. The square on the mean proportional is equal in area to the rectangle on the two radii vectors, and the mean proportional is therefore equivalent to the square root of the area of the rectangle.

In Fig. 3, we construct a rectangle AB, in any desired ratio of end to side, and draw a diagonal CD, and the diagonal of the reciprocal BE, at right angles to CD. We continue the angular spiral by drawing the lines EF, FG, GH, etc., parallel alternately to the ends and sides of the rectangle, toward the pole o of the spiral, which is at the intersection of the diagonals CD and BE, and then draw a freehand spiral around

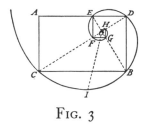

FIG. 3

the points C, B, D, E, F, G, H, etc. These are established points on the curve, which is the escribed spiral of the rectangle. The problem now is to describe the spiral correctly, and the method depends upon the

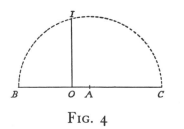

FIG. 4

finding of a mean proportional geometrically between two given lines. Let us assume, Fig. 4, that the two given lines are BO and OC of Fig. 3. We bisect BC at A, and with AB as radius describe a semicircle BIC; from the point o we erect a perpendicular to BC, which intersects the semicircle at ɪ. The line oɪ is a mean proportional to ʙo and oc, and is the length of the radius vector oɪ bisecting ʙoc of Fig. 3. By a continuation of this method we can obtain as many points on the curve as may be needed for its correct construction. In the large diagram Fig. 5, the rectangle is for greater convenience turned so that its diagonal cᴅ is horizontal. This horizontal line may be extended to

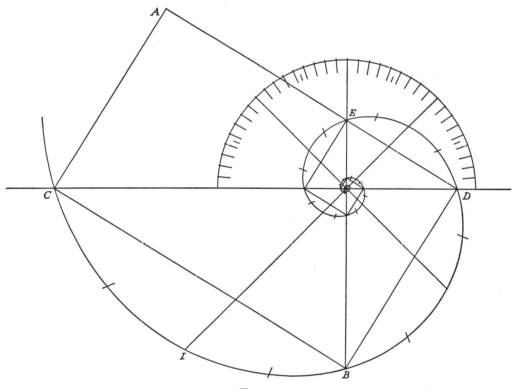

FIG. 5

any needed length, and the lengths of all established radii vectors marked thereon from the pole o. As shown in the diagram, a protractor may be used for bisecting the angles, or we may bisect them with a pair of dividers.

When the spiral has been accurately constructed and drawn on thin bristol board, it is cut out exactly with sharp shears, and slight inaccuracies corrected with fine sandpaper. As the curve approaches the pole a sharp penknife should be used, and great care exercised because of the constantly diminishing size of the spiral. The curve should not be cut too close to the pole however, as there is danger that the perforated eye may break through. It is essential that the eye should be exactly on the intersection of the two diagonals of the rectangle, and the perforation should not be larger than is sufficient to permit the use of a fairly strong needle, around which the instrument is to be rotated. Inaccuracies in the instrument may be detected by drawing the spiral, and then gradually rotating it and drawing other spirals close to it. If the instrument is not accurate the curves will not follow each other smoothly. When the bristol board curve is complete the instrument may be cut from sheet celluloid about 1-32 of an inch in thickness for small instruments, and proportionally thicker for larger instruments. The method used by the author was to use a large needle inserted in a handle of wood, and by repeatedly scribing the curve on the celluloid, around the bristol board curve, it was gradually cut through. The task may be facilitated by scribing upon both sides of the celluloid. The curve is then sandpapered in the same way as the bristol board instruments. A slight rounding of the edges is advisable, to prevent the ink from the ruling pen from running under the instrument and blotting. To prevent this, very little ink should be used in the pen at any time.

The necessary triangles for drawing the different rectangles are cut in the same way, and their use will greatly facilitate the making of designs and drawings in accordance with the principles of Dynamarhythmic Design. A metric scale may be used to measure the ratios, or the rectangles may be constructed accurately by the methods already shown. Should there be any demand for these tools, that demand will no doubt be eventually met by the manufacturers of drawing instruments.

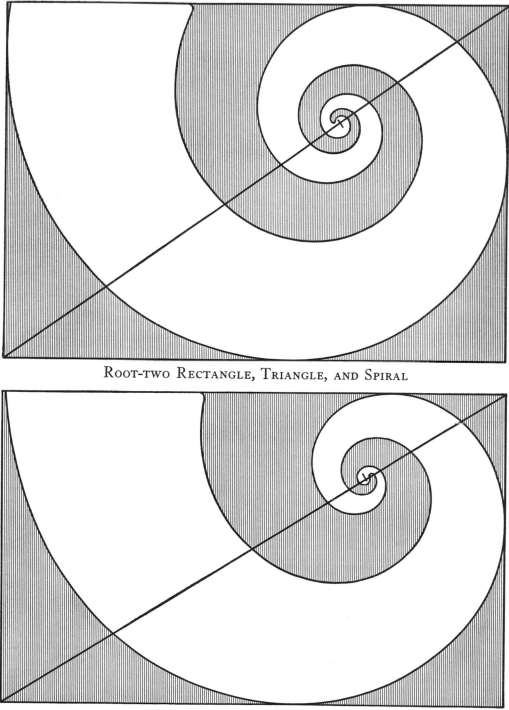

Root-two Rectangle, Triangle, and Spiral

1.618 Rectangle, Triangle, and Spiral

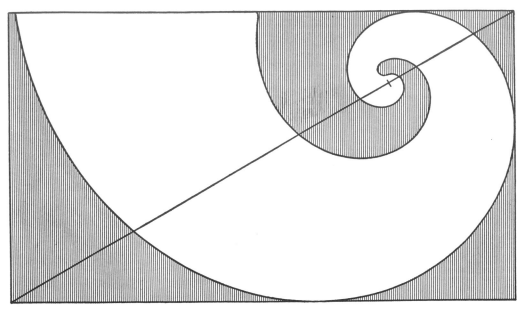

ROOT-THREE RECTANGLE, TRIANGLE, AND SPIRAL

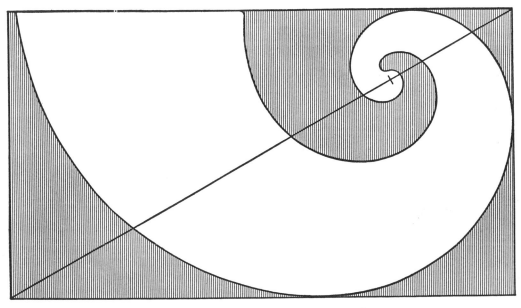

1.775 RECTANGLE, TRIANGLE, AND SPIRAL

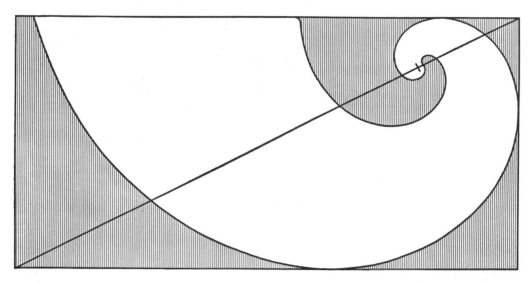

Root-four Rectangle, Triangle, and Spiral

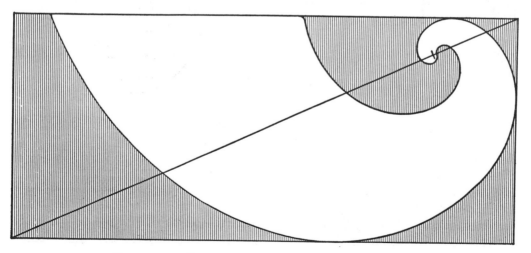

Root-five Rectangle, Triangle, and Spiral

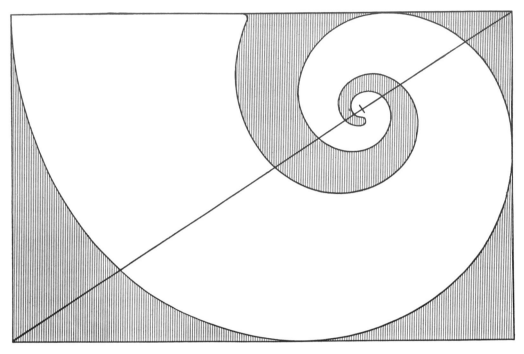

1.5388 RECTANGLE, TRIANGLE, AND SPIRAL

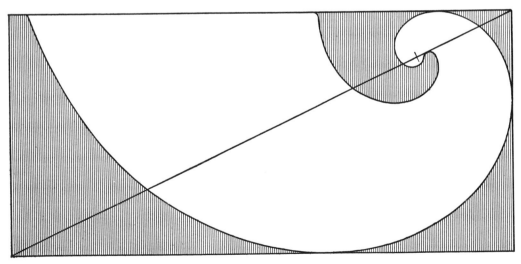

2.09 RECTANGLE, TRIANGLE, AND SPIRAL

CHAPTER IV

THE ROOT-TWO RECTANGLE

Fig. 1 is a square which represents a unit of area, therefore any one of its sides represents a unit of length, which may be an arbitrary

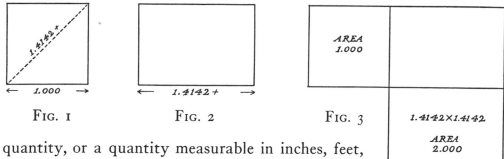

FIG. 1   FIG. 2   FIG. 3

1.4142×1.4142

AREA
2.000

quantity, or a quantity measurable in inches, feet, centimeters, meters, etc. Taking the diagonal of the square as the side and the unit of length as the end, we have a root-two rectangle, Fig. 2. The area of the square constructed on the end is one, and the area of the square on the side is two, as shown in Fig. 3. In this way, while the relationship of end to side is incommensurate, it is commensurate in square. (This property is common, with the regular exceptions, to all root-rectangles.) Geometrically the diagonal of a square is an exactly measurable line, but arithmetically its length cannot be stated exactly in relationship to the unit of length, as the fraction 1.4142+ is endless.

If we draw a diagonal AB to the root-two rectangle Fig. 4, and cross this diagonal at right angles CD, the point C, where the short diagonal cuts the side EB, is exactly half way between E and B, and therefore cuts the rectangle into two equal rectangles, each of which is a reciprocal of the parent rectangle. This is the only rectangle whose half is exactly equal in shape to the whole. The process of subdivision of the root-two rectangle into terms of root-two may be continued to infinity,

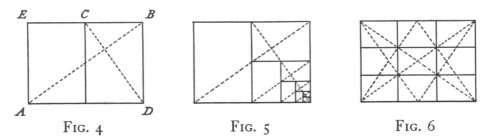

FIG. 4   FIG. 5   FIG. 6

as in Fig. 5. The rectangles may also be divided through the eyes or poles, at the crossing of the diagonals, as in Fig. 6. Lines drawn through the eyes divide the rectangle into three parts, both vertically and horizontally.

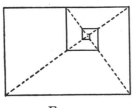

FIG. 7

Fig. 7 shows how the angular spiral may be drawn within the rectangle, starting from the pole, at the crossing of the diagonals, each turn of the spiral is in the continued ratio of 1 to 1.4142 or exactly 1.4142 times the preceding distance. The curved spiral, which is known as a logarithmic or equiangular spiral, may be inscribed within the rectangle, or escribed, as shown in Fig. 8. (The exact method is described in Chapter III.) In the case of the escribed spiral, the curve touches at all the exterior angles of the gnomonic triangles. The two shorter legs of each triangle are also in the ratio of 1 to 1.4142, and are called *the radii vectors* of the spiral. The exact points of tangency of the inscribed spiral with the sides of the rectangles are much more difficult to locate, and while the author was able to locate the points with sufficient

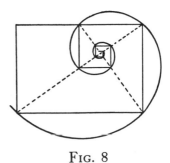

FIG. 8

accuracy for the practical purposes of design, his knowledge was unequal to the task of making an exact mathematical statement. To that end he submitted the matter to Mr. René Albrecht Carrié of the College of the City of New York, who has contributed a separate chapter on the subject.

The location of the point of tangency of the spiral within the rectangle must be known to make it possible to reverse the spiral without a break in the curve. In the root-two rectangle shown in Fig. 9, the author

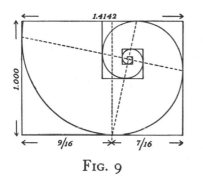

has located the point at 7/16 of the distance from the right end of the rectangle; the reverse would be true if the spiral were drawn from the opposite side. 7/16 of 1.4142 equals .6187. Mr. Carrié has figured the point of tangency at .6185, therefore the reversed spiral will fill approximately 7/8 of the rectangle.

Using a metric scale, ten centimeters is taken as representing unity; therefore the root-two rectangle is ten centimeters in height, and fourteen centimeters, one millimeter, and $\frac{42}{100}$ in length. The fraction .6185 is six centimeters, one millimeter and $\frac{85}{100}$ on the scale. The line or radius vector from the pole of the rectangle to the point of tangency in any rectangle, taken together with the base line of the rectangle, establishes the angle of the spiral. This angle is constant; that is, if a radius vector is drawn from the pole to any point on the spiral, and a line is drawn tangent to the spiral at that point, the angle formed by the two lines is always the same for that particular spiral. It is from this property of the curve that it takes the name of the equiangular, constant angle or logarithmic spiral. By means of this angle, the point of tangency may be established without measurements in any rectangle, drawn to any scale.

Fig. 10 shows the completed unit reversed face to face. Fig. 11 is the same unit reversed back to back. Fig. 12 shows two root-two spirals rotated at an angle of 180° to each other.

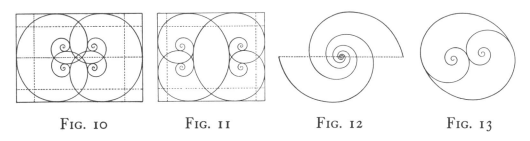

FIG. 10   FIG. 11   FIG. 12   FIG. 13

A property which is peculiar to the root-two spiral is shown in Fig. 13. Another root-two spiral may be drawn tangent to it at three points. If a tracing is made and superimposed upon the first spiral and rotated in such a way that the two spirals are continually in contact with each other, you will have the uncanny effect of the spirals being mutually swallowed by each other, like the two snakes of tradition. This is due to the fact that on adding a segment of the curve enclosing two successive gnomons each lying between two radii vectors at right angles to each other, Fig. 9, the width of the spiral is doubled.

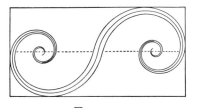

FIG. 14

Fig. 14 shows the construction of the root-two s-curve. From two poles lying on the axis the two spirals are drawn meeting at a point in the axis half way between. To increase the thickness of the s-curve, lines should be drawn on both sides equidistant from the center line. As the thickness of the curve is increased the distance between the poles is proportionally decreased, if the height is maintained. A continuation of this unit will produce the Greek wave design.

The octagon is intimately related to the root-two system as may be seen from Fig. 15. It is a compound figure composed of triangles representing halves of diagonally divided squares, root-two rectangles and a large square in the center which is twice the area of the complete squares in the corners of the enclosing square. The octagon has been used as a unit of design from the earliest times and has been an especially important element of Byzantine and Arabic art.

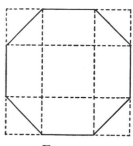

FIG. 15

The crossed root-two rectangles, Fig. 16, with their diagonals, result in a very interesting tile pattern. Repeat on dotted lines.

FIG. 16

CHAPTER V

ROOT-TWO RECTANGLE — PLATES AND DESCRIPTIONS

PLATE I

No. 1. Band exemplifying the simple proportional relationship of the root-two rectangle plus its reciprocal. These areas are harmoniously related because the smaller rectangle is just one-half of the larger rectangle and is of the same shape. The root-two rectangle is the only rectangle in which one half of the figure is similar in shape to the whole.

No. 2. The same diagram as No. 1 but with the diagonals indicated. Observe that the diagonals of the larger and of the smaller rectangles bear the same proportional relationship to each other, as does the end to the side of the root-two rectangle, or as 1 to 1.4142.

No. 3. Simple band composed of root-two rectangles with reciprocals of contrasting color.

No. 4. Same diagram as No. 3, but with the diagonals of the parent rectangle and of its reciprocal crossed at right angles. The resultant triangular forms are in the continued ratio of 1 to 1.4142 in line, and in area of 1:2:4:8, etc. It is obvious that this is also true of the rectangles.

No. 5. The diagonals of all the reciprocals have been drawn. The perpendiculars separating the reciprocals have been omitted, and only the diagonals stressed, resulting in the appearance of the root-two rectangles lying along the diagonals of the reciprocals.

No. 6. By the addition of still more diagonals, our band is subdivided into smaller root-two rectangles lying along the diagonals of the parent rectangles.

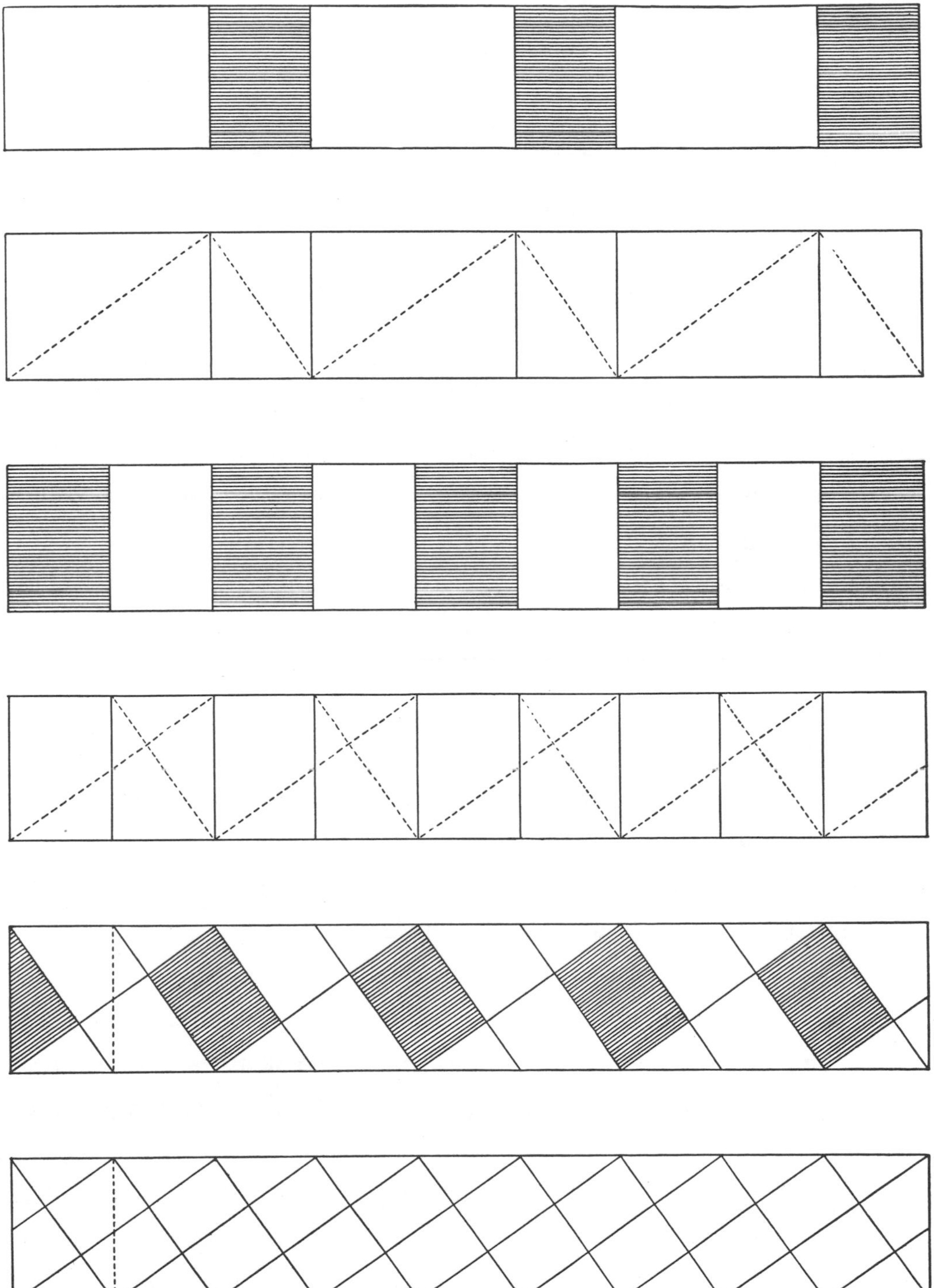

PLATE I

Root-two Rectangle — Plate II

No. 1. As in No. 1, Plate I, this band is composed of root-two rectangles, alternating with their reciprocals. Around the four poles of each rectangle, and of each reciprocal, are wound the angular spirals, so that each root-two rectangle and each reciprocal is completely filled by the four spirals. The width of the white bands compared with the black bands is arbitrary in this case, but may be varied to conform to any root-two relationship of ratios.

No. 2. In this band the root-two rectangle shows still further elaboration. With the dividing line between the rectangle and the reciprocal as an axis, the design of half of the reciprocal is reversed, and continued to meet in the center of the root-two rectangle the reversed half of the unit, while the interval is filled with four smaller root-two rectangles, each composed of two spirals. Observe that they exactly fill the space.

No. 3. In this design the root-two rectangles are lying along the diagonals of the reciprocals, and are interlaced.

No. 4. This band shows a somewhat similar interlacing of the design, but some of the spirals composing the rectangles have been eliminated, and a center line has been added to the white areas. Observe that the diagonal lines are always the diagonals of the rectangle or of its reciprocal.

No. 5. This design is very similar to the Greek fret or meander, except that in this case, the element of a proportionate increase of growth in the root-two ratio has been introduced. The diagonal of the

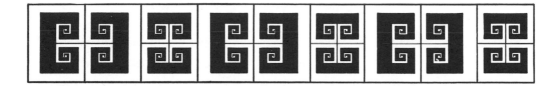

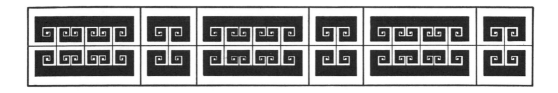

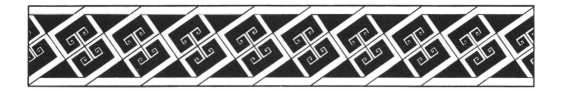

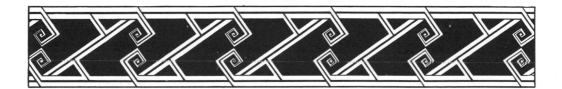

PLATE II

rectangle has been crossed in the center by the diagonal of its reciprocal, and the two spirals rotated at an angle of 180° to each other forming a continuous band, alternately increasing and decreasing in width
in the root-two ratio. The white and the black bands are in this instance of the same width, but may be varied as desired. If the diagonal
of the rectangle is drawn it will be observed that the band of white
separating each unit of the design is common to any two successive
units, so that the rectangles overlap to the extent of that band.

No. 6. Running band of spirals rotated at an angle of 180° from
the poles, along the diagonals of the rectangles, interrupted by diagonal
bands at right angles to, and in proportional relationship with, the
running spirals. This design may be made into an all-over pattern.

No. 1. In this design the angular double spiral forms in the reciprocal are joined by the diagonals of the parent rectangles forming a series of angular s-forms overlapping to the extent of the reciprocals.

No. 2. In the construction of this design the inner band is divided perpendicularly into root-two reciprocals, and horizontally into three parts. At the intersection of the reciprocal divisions with the horizontal divisions, the poles are placed alternately one-third of the distance from the bottom, and one-third of the distance from the top. From the poles are drawn the double angular spirals, lying along the diagonals of the reciprocals and joined into an angular s-form by the diagonals of the parent rectangles.

No. 3. Similar to the above design, except that the poles are on every other perpendicular division of the reciprocals. There is a striking resemblance in these designs to the designs of the Aztecs and the Mayans, except of course that their designs were lacking in the principles of proportionate growth. This similarity is not the result of conscious imitation, but has been caused by the logical development of the principles inherent in Dynamarhythmic Design.

No. 4. Double progression of double root-two angular spirals laid back to back. The diagonals are those of the root-two rectangles and of their reciprocals.

No. 5. Counterchange pattern formed of root-two rectangles divided into contrasting areas by their diagonals and also by horizontal and vertical lines through their centers. Each smaller root-two rectangle consists of a simple area contrasted with a similar area filled with its angular spiral, alternately black on white and white on black.

No. 6. Simple progression of root-two reciprocals in the upper part of every other one of which is its angular spiral joined to the next succeeding spiral by the diagonal of the upper part of the intervening reciprocal. The thickness of the spiral band controls the ratio of the black and white areas. This design is very reminiscent of Pompeian decoration.

PLATE III

ROOT-TWO RECTANGLE — PLATE IV

No. 1. Progression of angular spiral s-shapes each unit of which is composed of two spirals joined by a band lying along the diagonal of the root-two rectangle. The width of this connecting band is controlled by the diagonals of the half of the reciprocal areas intervening between successive spirals.

No. 2. In this design the diagonals of the reciprocals are divided into three parts, marking the position of the poles of the double angular spirals. The smaller black areas are root-two rectangles which are one-half or reciprocals of the larger intervening black area.

No. 3. Interlacing angular s-forms composed of two angular spirals joined by a band the length of which is controlled by the ends of the small adjoining rectangles.

No. 4. Band composed of reversed angular spirals interlocking with similar reversed spirals face to face. The spirals interlock to the extent of one-third of the combined spirals; or become tangent at a point half-way between the ends of the small rectangles formed by the spirals.

No. 5. This design seems very Chinese in character, although the pattern is almost entirely the result of the structure. The upper as well as the lower half of the band is composed of a succession of root-two rectangles, with the angular spirals reversed end to end. On the dividing line of the adjoining rectangles the spirals are repeated, with smaller supplementary spirals filling the space between the inner spirals and the outer bands.

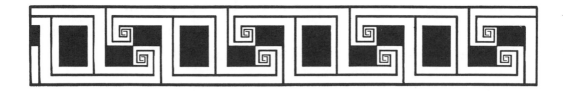

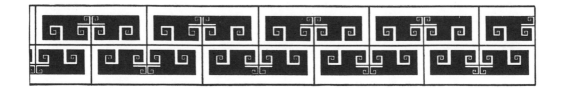

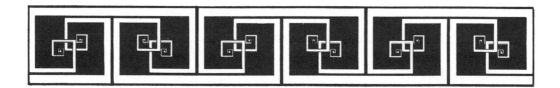

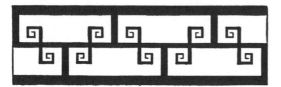

Plate IV

No. 6. Design composed of an alternating progression of units above and below composed of a plain root-two area adjoined by two reciprocal areas reversed; each reciprocal area composed of an angular spiral, the joining of the upper spirals with the lower, forms the angular s-shapes which join the upper part of the band to the lower.

No. 7. Progression of upright angular s-forms in which the wide ends of the white spirals join on the center line of the band.

Root-two Rectangle — Plate V

No. 1. Each root-two rectangle in the pattern is divided into two reciprocals of contrasting color which alternate throughout the design. Each reciprocal is composed of two smaller reciprocals of the same color, in which the angular spiral of the rectangle is opposed by the spiral lying along the diagonals, forming a series of triangles in the ratio of $1 : 2 : 4 : 8$, etc.

No. 2. Counterchange pattern somewhat similar to the above. In this case, however, the contrasting spiral forms lie alternately along the edges of the rectangles, and along the diagonals of each individual reciprocal. The units of the lower band are not placed directly under those of the upper part, but each unit is centered on the dividing line of two units in the upper part or vice versa.

No. 3. Counterchange pattern composed of reciprocals with their angular spirals of contrasting color. In each reciprocal two spirals of contrasting color are wrapped around the pole. Each spiral modified by a band of contrasting color.

No. 4. A tile pattern of Moorish aspect in which the root-two rectangle is divided by its diagonals, and the diagonals of its reciprocals. Each reciprocal is likewise divided until each root-two rectangle is divided into four rectangles, each one divided by its diagonals. The resulting structural network is then filled with contrasting color.

No. 5. The band consists of a series of triangles in the ratio of $1 : 4 : 8 : 16$, etc., caused by the logical subdivision of the root-two rectangles into triangles. The band is first divided into root-two reciprocals side by side, each reciprocal is divided by its long diagonals into four parts, by a continued subdivision and the suppression of some of the structural lines, and filling the areas with contrasting color the design is formed. An inspection of the design in most cases will make the matter simple of comprehension, while the description is necessarily complicated and very confusing.

No. 6. In this design the curved spiral first appears. It is contrasted with the angular spiral, both rotated about the pole in the center of the rectangle, and placed on a background of contrasting color, each spiral modified with a center line. The student will learn more by redrawing these designs, than he will from any description. By observing closely the diagonal lines the structure may ordinarily be recovered. Notice that in most cases where the spirals are continuous, that the rectangular part of the structure encroaches to some extent on the contiguous rectangle, but that the extent of the encroachment is in proportion to the theme of the design.

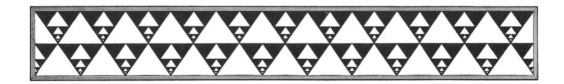

PLATE V

No. 1. Reversed root-two units interlaced to the extent of one revolution of the curve. A complete revolution of the curve comprises four gnomons, each of which lies between any two radii vectors at right angles to each other.

No. 2. Same design as No. 1, reversed and interlaced face to face.

No. 3. Same reversed spiral unit, interlacing alternately face to face, and back to back, to the extent of one revolution of the spiral.

No. 4. Similar to No. 2, except that in this instance the curves are interlaced in each case triangularly.

No. 5. Two bands like No. 1, interlaced back to back. Other combinations of these units will suggest themselves to the ingenious student. They may for example be joined together at an angle to each other; they may also be combined to cover a surface.

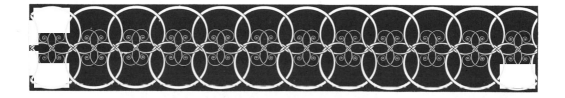

PLATE VI

No. 1. Doubly reversed curved spiral alternating with the similar unit, of doubly reversed angular spirals.

No. 2. Root-two spirals rotated at an angle of 180° to each other from the poles on the axis, the spirals changing from a curved to a straight line which continues to the side of the band, in turn forming a root-two angular spiral, which is joined to the next unit by the angular s-shape formed by rotating the angular spiral at an angle of 180°.

No. 3. Similar to No. 2, but the spirals end where the curve would, as in No. 2, change into a straight line, and an angular spiral is formed at right angles to the curved spiral. The proportions are so finely adjusted that there is just room for the interlacing of the adjoining unit.

No. 4. The structure of this design is somewhat difficult to explain. The s-shaped units are joined end to end in a small root-two rectangle; the poles of the separate units are at the intersections of the diagonals of this rectangle, the curves coming tangent with its inner sides, and also tangent with the inner sides of the opposing units. At the point where the two spirals join, forming the double s-shape spiral unit, is placed the center line of a root-two reciprocal; within the confines of this reciprocal are formed the angular spirals which are a continuation of the curved spirals forming the s-shape.

No. 5. Spiral units, rotated at an angle of 180° alternating with angular spiral units rotated at the same angle. The background is filled with detail of a somewhat Baroque character, merely to show how ornament of a free character may be added to a structural base.

PLATE VII

CHAPTER VI

THE WHIRLING SQUARE RECTANGLE (1.618)

The whirling square rectangle is a special case of the rectangles of the whirling gnomons. It is in the ratio of extreme and mean proportion, 1 to 1.618+, and is the so-called divine section of Pythagoras, who taught that the universe is ordered by mathematical regularities and constancies. In extreme and mean proportion, the lesser term is to the greater, as the greater is to the sum of the lesser plus the greater; $1.618 \div 1, = 1.618$; $1 + 1.618 = 2.618$; $2.618 \div 1.618 = 1.618$. A close approximation of this ratio may be arrived at by a summation series as follows: $1 + 1 = 2$, $1 + 2 = 3$, $2 + 3 = 5$, $3 + 5 = 8$, $5 + 8 = 13$, $8 + 13 = 21$, $13 + 21 = 34$, $21 + 34 = 55$, etc. This is an infinite series, and when the higher terms are divided one into the other, the ratio is always 1.618 more or less. This is known as the *Fibonacci Series* and was first mentioned in the writings of Leonardo Pisano, a celebrated Italian mathematician of the thirteenth century, who was called Fibonacci. This series is intimately connected with the growth of plants and of seed and leaf distribution. It was noticed by Kepler in the early part of the seventeenth century, by the German botanists Schimper and Braun in 1835, and the French botanist Bravais in 1837. The subject is also treated in a scholarly way by Professor A. H. Church in his work on Phyllotaxis,[1] and is discussed by Theodore A. Cook,[2] and also by D'Arcy W. Thompson.[3]

[1] *Relation of Phyllotaxis to Mechanical Laws* (Oxford, 1901, 1903).　[2] *The Curves of Life* (New York, Henry Holt and Company, 1914).　[3] *Growth and Form* (Cambridge: at the University Press, 1917).

From the earliest times the ratio of extreme and mean proportion has had considerable mystic significance. Prop. 11, Book II of Euclid, Fig. 1, shows how this ratio may be obtained geometrically. AB is a given straight line. On AB is described the square ACBD, a side of which is bisected at E; E and B are joined and the line CA is produced to F, EF being equal to EB. On AF is described the square AFGH. AB is divided at H into extreme and mean proportion, as is also the line FC at A. If this

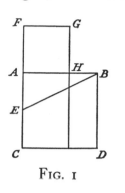

FIG. 1

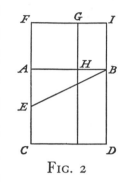

FIG. 2

construction is completed by producing FG to I, and DB to I as in Fig. 2, we have a whirling square rectangle. The author's method of producing this rectangle is also shown herewith in Fig. 3. Let ABCD be a square of any size, bisect BD at E and describe the semicircle BFD. Draw the diagonal CE produced to F and with CF as a radius describe the arc FG meeting CD produced to G; complete the rectangle AHCG.

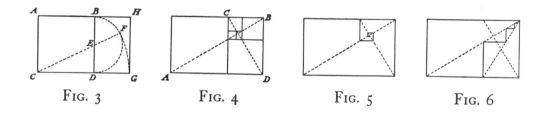

FIG. 3   FIG. 4   FIG. 5   FIG. 6

Fig. 4 is the whirling square rectangle complete with its diagonals indicated, and shows how the squares or gnomons revolve to infinity around the pole, as shown in Fig. 6 on page 5. The smaller rectangle CD is the reciprocal of AB. The construction of the 1.618+ angular spiral is shown in Fig. 5, and the method of constructing the scale of ratios of end to side of the rectangle is shown in Fig. 6.

The point of tangency of the spiral of the 1.618 rectangle is .6687 distant from the right end of the rectangle, Fig. 7. If the spiral is re-

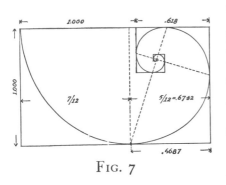

FIG. 7

versed on an axis corresponding to this point, and rotated at an angle of 180°, Fig. 8, the rotated spiral will interlace with the small spiral near the pole of the reversed half of the unit. This is not satisfactory, as it does not allow sufficient room for a spiral band of any considerable thickness to pass through the small spiral; if however, the axis of the unit is taken at a point .6742 or 5/12 distant from the end of the rectangle, the rotated spiral comes tangent with the small inner spiral (reference to the figure will make this clear) and allows sufficient room for a band of some thickness to interlace with the larger spirals. The discrepancy is only 55/1000 of the length of the rectangle, and at a small scale is scarcely perceptible. This unit may

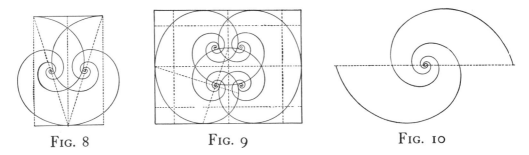

FIG. 8   FIG. 9   FIG. 10

be formed into a continuous band by joining with similar units on the axes. The doubly reversed spiral is shown in Fig. 9. This unit may be interlaced end to end, or side to side, with similar units on the axes indicated by the dotted lines, or made into a surface pattern. Fig. 10 shows the spiral rotated at an angle of 180° around the pole. The s-curve is constructed in the same way as the root-two s-curve.

CHAPTER VII

WHIRLING SQUARE RECTANGLE (1.618) — PLATES AND DESCRIPTIONS

PLATE I

No. 1. The simple proportional relationship of the 1.618 rectangle alternated with its reciprocal. The diagonal of the rectangle is joined to that of the reciprocal at right angles, making a continuous line throughout the length of the band.

No. 2. In this band the 1.618 rectangle is divided into its simplest proportional relationship of a square, or the gnomon, and the reciprocal of the rectangle, by the crossing of the diagonal of the entire rectangle with that of the reciprocal, at right angles. The reciprocal can be divided in a like manner, and the process continued to infinity.

No. 3. Here both diagonals of the rectangle are drawn, as well as the diagonals of the reciprocals at both ends of the rectangle, forming a net-work of squares and 1.618 rectangles when lines are drawn through the intersections of the diagonals, parallel to the ends and sides of the rectangle. The method is shown at the right of the band. The process of subdivision may be continued to infinity.

No. 4. In this band small intersecting 1.618 rectangles are drawn lying along the diagonals of the reciprocals. By the suppression or logical addition of lines of construction many suggestions are developed for the making of designs. The right end of the band shows additional divisions. Observe that all of the areas are either squares or

1.618 rectangles, or the halves of 1.618 rectangles, in proportional relationship to each other.

No. 5. At the junction of two successive rectangles are drawn two smaller intersecting 1.618 rectangles, lying along the diagonals of the larger rectangles. The smaller rectangles are each divided into a square, or gnomon of the rectangle, and a reciprocal, the combination of the two intersecting rectangles forming a third rectangle at right angles to both. The diagonal of the third rectangle, which is here suppressed, is the dividing line between successive rectangles or units of the band.

No. 6. In this diagram a succession of small rectangles lying along the diagonals of the reciprocals is drawn, each in turn divided into squares and 1.618 rectangles (or gnomons and reciprocals), and reversed, so that two squares adjoin, forming a root-four rectangle which gives a third proportional element in the design.

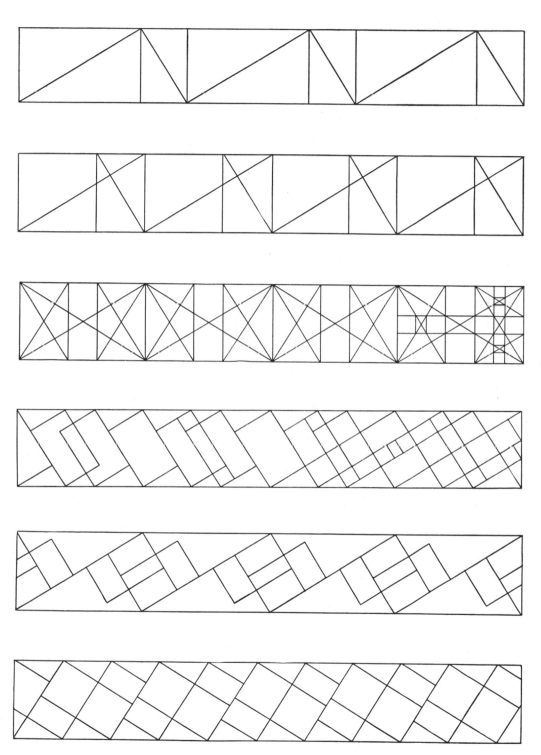

PLATE I

Whirling Square Rectangle — Plate II

No. 1. Tile pattern consisting of alternating areas of the 1.618 rectangle and its reciprocal in contrasting colors.

No. 2. Alternating squares or gnomons of the 1.618 rectangle and of its reciprocal in contrasting colors.

No. 3. Reciprocal of the 1.618 rectangle divided into gnomon and reciprocal in contrasting colors, joined together with like reciprocals with the contrasting areas alternately at top and bottom of the band.

No. 4. Reciprocal of the 1.618 rectangle divided into gnomon and reciprocal, which reciprocal area is again divided into gnomon and reciprocal, joined together with like units with contrasting areas alternately at top and bottom of the design.

No. 5. 1.618 rectangle divided into gnomon and reciprocal, the reciprocal in turn divided into gnomon and reciprocal, joined to similar units subdivided in like manner.

No. 6. The unit of this design is a 1.618 rectangle divided into gnomon and reciprocal; the reciprocal again divided into areas, in contrasting colors, consisting of a reciprocal at each end and the intervening area divided into two squares and a 1.618 rectangle.

No. 7. In this pattern the diagonals of the 1.618 rectangle and the diagonals of its reciprocals mark the points on the ends and sides of the rectangle where the lines parallel to the ends and sides are drawn, cutting the rectangle into alternate squares and 1.618 rectangles. The repeat in this instance is a square, plus an area consisting of two small 1.618 rectangles and a small square.

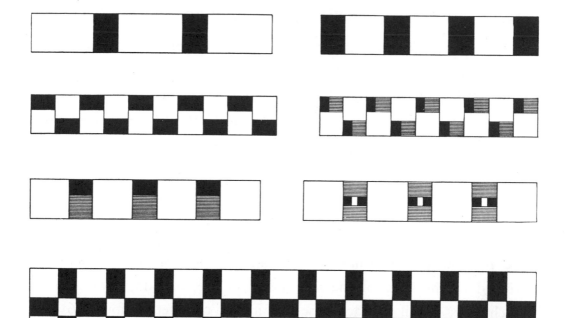
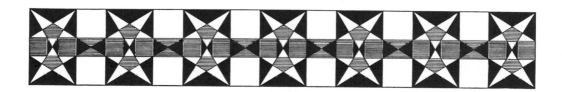

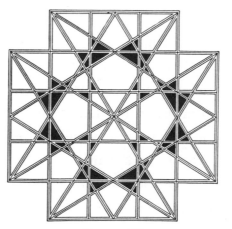

PLATE II

No. 8. The rectangle is divided as in No. 7 by the diagonals of the rectangle and by those of its reciprocals and by lines parallel to the ends and sides of the rectangle into triangles, squares, and irregular pentagons, all in proportional relationship. Here the repeat is a square.

No. 9. Tile design constructed by crossing two 1.618 rectangles at right angles in a square. This divides the area into a large square in the center and four small squares in the corners, with four rectangular areas between, each of which consists of two 1.618 rectangles. In the large square in the center is inscribed a smaller square at an angle of 45° to it, which is just half the area, and the sides of this square are continued to the sides of the containing square, marking two points on each side, which in each case are joined completing four 1.618 rectangles. On each end of these rectangles are placed the reciprocals, and from opposite poles are drawn angular spirals; additional angular spirals are rotated from the same poles, coinciding with the sides of the small squares in the corners of the design. A smaller square is inscribed in the center at an angle of 45° to the escribed square, and the areas filled with contrasting colors.

No. 10. Lattice work pattern constructed by crossing two 1.618 rectangles at right angles. In each rectangle are drawn its diagonals and the diagonals of its reciprocals, as well as the lines parallel to the ends and sides of the rectangles, which divide the rectangles into gnomons and reciprocals. Parts of the background are filled in, in black, accentuating the irregular octagonal form in the center.

No. 11. Tile pattern constructed in a similar way to No. 10, with additional subdivisions of the rectangular areas at the sides of the enclosing square. Each of these consists of two 1.618 rectangles. The lines parallel to the ends and sides of the crossed rectangles, which mark the divisions between gnomons and reciprocals, are omitted.

Whirling Square Rectangle — Plate III

No. 1. In this pattern the gnomons, which in the 1.618 rectangle are squares, are shown whirling around the pole in the continued ratio in line, of extreme and mean proportion, 1 to 1.618; or in area, in the ratio of 1 to 2.618. The lines on each side of the band are arbitrary and are used merely for contrast.

No. 2. To construct this design the diagonals of the 1.618 rectangle are drawn, as well as those of its reciprocals. These diagonals are used merely in the construction of the design and do not appear in the finished drawing. When the reciprocals have both been drawn, we have an area in the center of the rectangle, which represents the extent to which the squares on each end of the rectangle overlap each other, and which also represents the area between the reciprocals. At the intersections of the diagonals of the 1.618 rectangle with the inner sides of the reciprocals, in the center area are drawn the squares, which are continued to the corners of the rectangle between the diagonals of the parent rectangle and those of the reciprocals. The decrease in area is in the ratio of 2.618 to 1.000. These squares in reality will never reach the corners.

No. 3. In this design the repeat is also a 1.618 rectangle, divided into a reciprocal and a gnomon; in the square or gnomon are placed four reciprocals overlapping each other, and forming a square in the center, which is filled in, in black; from the four corners of this square are drawn diagonal lines to the four corners of the gnomon, as described in No. 2, and the squares drawn in a constantly decreasing ratio of

2.618 to 1.000, to the corners. The reciprocal is subdivided in the same way as the repeat of No. 2. When added to the gnomon this forms the repeat. The band running through the center of the design is composed of squares alternating with 1.618 rectangles and root-four rectangles composed of two adjoining gnomons.

No. 4. The rectangles overlap to the extent of a reciprocal. The reciprocals in turn have a reciprocal on each end and from two poles of each are drawn their angular spirals; supplementary spirals are then drawn from the same poles at an angle of 45° to the first spirals and, when continued through to the sides and ends of the parent rectangle, partly enclose 1.618 rectangles. When the background is filled in, in black or color, the design is complete. The ratio of increase in area of the triangles is the same as that of the squares, 1 to 2.618.

No. 5. In this design, small 1.618 rectangles similar to the reciprocals in No. 4 are drawn at an angle of 45° to the base of the band, alternately reversed and touching each other. The centers of the rectangles between their reciprocals are continued through to the sides of the band, and the alternate areas filled in, in black or color. The units composing the pattern are 1.618 rectangles, squares, root-four rectangles and right-angled triangles, all in proportional relationship.

No. 6. The unit of this pattern is composed of two 1.618 rectangles overlapping at right angles to each other, with the decreasing squares common to both rectangles; some of the squares running horizontally have been omitted. The units are then reversed top to bottom and joined. Be careful in drawing these or similar patterns, that the black areas do not encroach upon the white, as there is a tendency to draw the black lines through the pattern; if this is not corrected the relationships of areas of black and white will not be correct. In all cases the pattern should be the logical result of the structural theme.

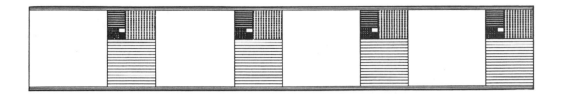

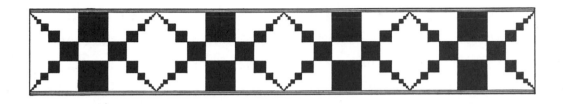

PLATE III

WHIRLING SQUARE RECTANGLE — PLATE IV

No. 1. This design is based on the construction shown in No. 4 of Plate I. The intersecting 1.618 rectangles come tangent in the center on the long diagonal of the parent rectangle; from the poles are drawn angular spirals which terminate in the corners of the repeat. Diagonals are drawn from the successive angles of the spirals to the corners of the rectangles, and in the rectangle common to adjoining units of the band is drawn a diagonal separating the repeating units, and one diagonal to each of its reciprocals.

No. 2. To construct this design, first draw one diagonal to the parent rectangle, and cross it at right angles with one diagonal of each of its reciprocals; draw a line cutting the rectangle into its reciprocal and its gnomon, with the gnomon to the right. Next draw the smaller 1.618 rectangles lying along the diagonals of the reciprocals, so that when the unit is repeated the gnomons of two of these rectangles adjoin each other. The lines cutting the smaller rectangles into gnomon and reciprocals are continued through from side to side of the band, parallel to the long diagonal of the parent rectangles. From one pole of each of the reciprocals of the smaller rectangles are drawn angular spirals. Additional lines are drawn perpendicular to the base of the band at intersections of some of the diagonals, and parts of the background are filled with free ornament somewhat Greek in character using the 1.618 spiral for the dominant curves. Some of the structural lines are omitted in the finished design.

No. 3. To produce this pattern, we superimpose the design shown in No. 5, Plate I, on a similar design, shifting the ends of the units of

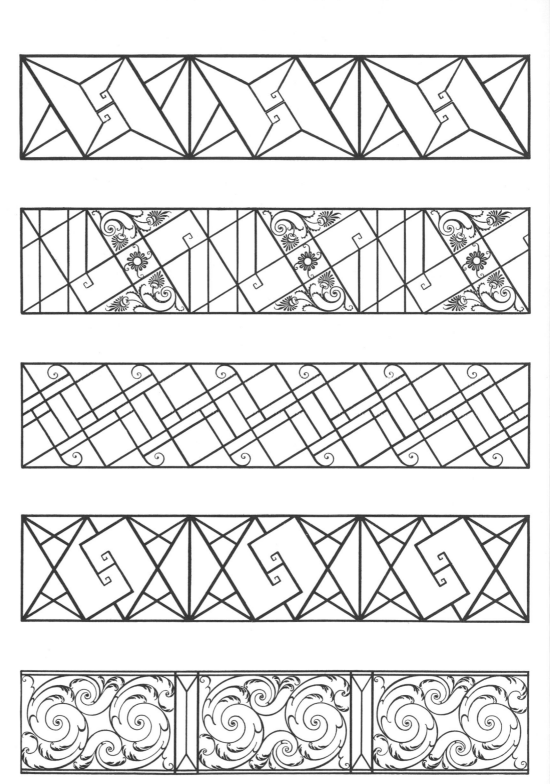

PLATE IV

the superimposed design to the centers of the underlying units. Small 1.618 spirals are used to tie up with the sides of the band.

No. 4. Here the design is similar in construction to No. 1, except that the diagonals of both reciprocals have been drawn, and the long diagonals of the parent rectangle have been drawn partly through. The angular spirals of the two rectangles lying along the diagonals of the reciprocals interlock in the center of the parent rectangle.

No. 5. From two poles lying on the horizontal axes of each unit of this design, are drawn 1.618 spirals at an angle of 180° to each other. Meeting these spirals are smaller spirals coming from the opposite direction. Free foliation has been added, following the spiral curves rhythmically. The rectangular areas between the repeats are each composed of three 1.618 rectangles, in which are drawn triangles, the sides of which are 1.618 diagonals. These triangles are connected by a line in the center of the area. This design shows a somewhat free application of the principles of Dynamarhythmic Design.

All of the designs on this plate are intended to show how Dynamarhythmic Design may be applied to iron work.

WHIRLING SQUARE RECTANGLE — PLATE V

No. 1. From poles lying on the horizontal axis of the band, are drawn two 1.618 spirals from opposite poles meeting on the axis, forming the s-shaped unit. The successive units are placed tangent to each other, and the poles of each two units are connected by the angular s-shape formed by two angular spirals drawn from the poles. If the width of the s-shaped band is increased, it decreases the distance between the poles of the successive units. If the width of the band is increased sufficiently, the smaller whorls will touch or may be made to interlace.

No. 2. Here one half of the s-unit is drawn entirely above the horizontal axis of the band, and the other half entirely below, and the poles of successive units connected by smaller s-curves. Upon the width of the bands of the s-curves will depend the distance between the poles of successive units, as in No. 1.

No. 3. From a horizontal band at the bottom of this design are drawn a succession of overlapping 1.618 spirals, which interlace and come tangent to a like succession of spirals growing from the top band. The space between successive spirals is governed by the width of the spiral bands, and also by the small s-curve which joins the poles of the upper and lower halves of the design. This s-curve is tangent to the upper and lower spirals.

No. 4. Draw a 1.618 rectangle, and one diagonal to it from the lower left corner to the upper right; draw a reciprocal in the center of the rectangle, and draw a diagonal to it crossing the diagonal of the parent rectangle at right angles. From the pole established by the intersection of the diagonals, draw the angular spirals at an angle of 180° to each other through to the sides of the band; curved spirals are then rotated at an angle of 180° from the same poles, joining with like spirals on the horizontal axis forming the s-curves. The angular spirals must be accurately gaged to allow the curved spirals to become tangent with the sides and corners of the angular spirals. No set rule can be given for this. The repeat is established by the distance between the two poles of the s-curve.

No. 5. To construct this design, first draw the 1.618 rectangle with a horizontal and a vertical axis. The rectangle is now divided into four small rectangles. Draw the diagonal of the rectangle from the upper left corner to the lower right corner. Then draw the diagonal of the lower left hand rectangle, from the upper left corner to the lower right corner, and the diagonal of its reciprocal on the left, and draw also the diagonal of the upper right hand rectangle, from upper left corner to the lower right corner, and the diagonal of its reciprocal to the right. At the intersection of these diagonals we have now established two points which are normally the poles of the 1.618 spirals within the rectangle; we must, however, allow for the thickness of the spiral band, so we must move the poles toward the minor axis of the parent rectangle, a distance corresponding to one half the width of the band, and from these diagonally opposite poles we draw the spirals meeting on the minor axis and forming the s-curve. In the center of the parent rectangle we now draw a reciprocal rectangle, with a diagonal from its upper left to its lower right corner. We now continue the upper and lower spirals of the s-curve horizontally to meet the opposite sides of the reciprocal, and vertically to meet the diagonal of the parent rectangle, from which points we draw diagonals at right angles to that of the reciprocal, and complete the angular spirals. From the same poles we rotate supple-

PLATE V

mentary angular spirals which meet and continue to the center forming an angular s-shape. From the poles of the curved spirals we next draw smaller spirals which meet the major axis of the rectangle at the sides of the reciprocal, and are continued along the major axis to meet in the center. The unit is now complete, and is joined with similar units to form the continued design.

Whirling Square Rectangle — Plate VI

No. 1. The 1.618 spirals are drawn from poles lying on the horizontal axis of the band and are reversed on a vertical axis corresponding to a point 5/12 of the distance from the end of the rectangle in which the pole of the spiral is located. The actual point of tangency, as has already been mentioned in the description of Fig. 8, is 55/1000 of the length of the 1.618 rectangle, nearer the side. The spirals are then rotated at an angle of 180° from the same poles. The width of the spiral bands is arbitrary in this design.

No. 2. This design is made with the doubly reversed unit shown in Fig. 9, which is interlaced side by side with similar units on the axes. The thickness of the spiral bands should come within the spiral in these designs and is regulated by the interlacing. If the bands are too wide they cannot pass through the interlacing of the smaller whorls of the spirals.

No. 3. This design is similar in construction to No. 3, Plate IV of the Root-three Rectangle. The 1.618 s-shaped units are each crossed by two similar curves which are alike in the angle of their inclination. The terminations of each two reversed s-curves interlace, and become tangent with each other and with the sides of the triangular areas between two crossed units. The dissimilarity in appearance of this design with the root-three design is due to the difference in the curves. The author can give no definite rule for the construction of this pattern, as the width of the bands controls the inclination of the curves, so that the result is largely a matter of experiment.

No. 4. To construct this design draw a 1.618 rectangle with two long diagonals, and both diagonals of a reciprocal on each end. Draw a horizontal and a vertical axis through the intersection of the major diagonals. The rectangle is now divided into an irregular hexagon in the center and two triangles forming x-shapes on either side. Add exteriorly to the width of the bands forming the top and bottom of the design, and also to the diagonals of the reciprocals, also exterior to the rectangle. In the center hexagon are grouped four 1.618 s-shaped curves, and branching from each are small 1.618 spirals, diminishing in size toward the center. A diamond drawn with 1.618 diagonals is placed in the center. The reciprocals on each end of the rectangle are common to two successive repeats.

No. 5. In this design the band is divided into three parts by two horizontal lines, on which are located the poles of the 1.618 spirals rotated at an angle of 180° to each other, which are reversed and interlaced on the horizontal axis, forming one half of the repeat, which is completed by reversing on a vertical axis. The free Renaissance ornament is added to show how the structure may be enriched if desired.

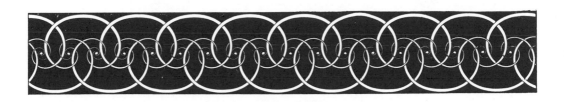

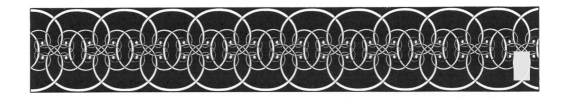

PLATE VI

CHAPTER VIII

THE ROOT-THREE RECTANGLE

If an area is to be completely covered by the juxtaposition of regular figures, these figures must be either squares, equilateral triangles or regular hexagons. Four squares may be grouped around a point, three hexagons, or six equilateral triangles, which in themselves form a hexagon, as in Fig. 1. The reason for this is simple, as the sum of the

FIG. 1

angles around a point equals four right angles or 360°, and the angles of a square being 90°, the angles of a hexagon 120°, and those of an equilateral triangle 60°, they will group themselves respectively, four, three, and six times around a point. The hexagon is the figure adopted by nature as the most economical in its space-filling properties. The bee, with the precision of an engineer, builds the honeycomb of hexagonal cells. Molecules, normally round, are, under the influence of atmospheric pressure compressed into hexagons.

If two equilateral triangles are placed side by side, and enclosed in a rectangle, as in Fig. 2, that rectangle will be root-three; that is,

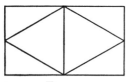

FIG. 2

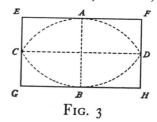

FIG. 3

the relationship of end to side will be as one to the square root of three, 1 to 1.732+, and the area of the square on the side of the rectangle will be three times that of the square on the end.

A simple and direct method of constructing a root-three rectangle is to draw a perpendicular line of the length of its unit side AB, as in Fig. 3, and describe two arcs, CAD and CBD, with the points B and A as centers. Through the points of intersection C and D of the arcs draw a line CD. Parallel to CD draw the lines EF and GH through A and B. Through the points of intersection C and D draw likewise the perpendiculars EG and FH parallel to AB and at right angles to EF and GH. This is simply an application of Prop. 1, Book I, of Euclid.

The diagonal of a root-three rectangle AB, Fig. 4, when crossed with a diagonal CD at right angles to it, from the opposite corner cuts

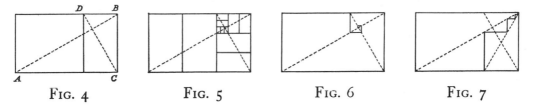

FIG. 4   FIG. 5   FIG. 6   FIG. 7

off the reciprocal DC, which is exactly of the same shape, and one third of the area of the parent rectangle. The rectangle may also be divided into four parts through the poles, each part consisting of a root-three rectangle plus its reciprocal. If the division is continued in height as well as in length it will result in sixteen small root-three rectangles.

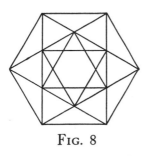

FIG. 8

The gnomons of the root-three rectangle are in each instance composed of two root-three rectangles side by side, so that by the continuous addition to the side of a root-three rectangle of its gnomon you will increase its size to infinity with no alteration of its shape, Fig. 5. This is true, in fact, of any rectangle. Fig. 6 shows the root-three angular spiral, and Fig. 7 how to construct the scale of ratios of end to side of the root-three rectangle.

If you join the opposite sides of a hexagon, Fig. 8, by parallel lines you will have three root-three rectangles crossing each other, forming a smaller hexagon in the center, one-third of the area of the large hexagon, which may be divided in the same way, and the process continued to infinity.

The spiral of the root-three rectangle comes tangent to the base line of the rectangle at a point approximately 2/5 of the distance from

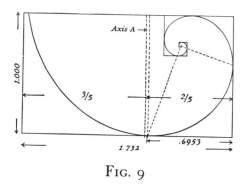

FIG. 9

the end, Fig. 9. The actual point of contact is .6953; 2/5 of 1.732 = .6928, a difference of .0025 or one quarter of a millimeter, when the rectangle is drawn with a metric scale, and ten centimeters represent unity.

Fig. 10 shows the spiral doubly reversed on the axes established by the points of tangency. The reciprocal spiral, at an angle of 90° to the parent spiral, and forming part of it, is rotated at an angle of 180° establishing the minor axis of the figure,

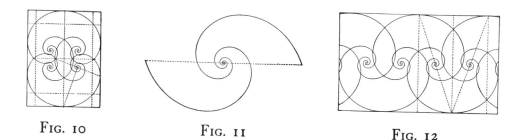

FIG. 10   FIG. 11   FIG. 12

on which both spirals are reversed, forming half of the unit; which is again reversed on the major axis, completing the figure. The four poles, from which this design is generated, mark the four corners of a root-three rectangle. The spirals rotated around the pole at an angle of

180° is shown in Fig. 11. By reversing Fig. 11 on the axes defined by the points of tangency, a running band is formed as shown in Fig. 12. A curious fact, for which the author has been unable to account, is that the rectangle occupied by the unit is a root-two rectangle. Half of the unit occupies a root-eight rectangle. Consequently the radius vector from the pole of a root-three spiral to the point of tangency has the same angle of inclination as the diagonal of a root-eight rectangle.

In the designs, the author has considered the center line as structural, and has added spirals on both sides to increase the thickness of the spiral bands. To be thoroughly consistent, special spirals should be used for this purpose, but for the practical purpose of working designs, the same curve may, with slight modifications in the drawing, be made to answer the purpose.

In order to produce the unit shown in Fig. 13 with the root-three spiral, the axis of the figure has to be moved somewhat further away from the side of the rectangle than the point of tan-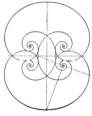gency, as shown in Fig. 9, axis A, in order to permit the reciprocal spirals to come tangent instead of interlacing with the smaller spirals as in Fig. 10. This causes a slight flattening of the curve at the point where the halves of the unit are reversed. The correct curve

FIG. 13

for this design is the spiral of the 1.775 rectangle, which forms the design perfectly.

CHAPTER IX

ROOT-THREE RECTANGLE — PLATES AND DESCRIPTIONS

PLATE I

No. 1. Band showing the simple proportional relationship of the root-three rectangle, and of its reciprocal. At the right side of the diagram the root-three rectangle is shown divided into three reciprocals each of which is the same shape as the parent figure but at right angles to it.

No. 2. Same as No. 1, except that the diagonals of the root-three rectangle and of its reciprocal are drawn. The diagonals of the reciprocals are at right angles to those of the rectangles.

No. 3. In this band the reciprocals are shown within the parent rectangles. In this case the band is composed of the gnomons of the rectangles, alternating with the reciprocals. It will be observed that in the root-three rectangle, the gnomon is composed of two reciprocals.

No. 4. The units of this band are root-three rectangles divided into three reciprocals, with the diagonals of the rectangles, crossed by the diagonals of the reciprocals on the ends of the units. This design is characterized by the appearance of small root-three rectangles formed by the joining of two units, and lying along the diagonals of the reciprocals.

No. 5. Similar to No. 4, with additional diagonals causing the appearance of the regular hexagon in the center of each unit rectangle.

No. 6. This design shows a succession of root-three reciprocals in each of which are drawn its diagonals and the diagonals of all three of its divisions, forming a net-work of regular hexagons, of diamonds, and of root-three rectangles, all in proportional relationship to each other.

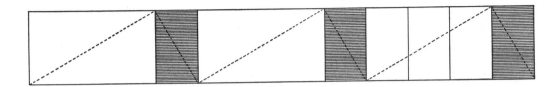

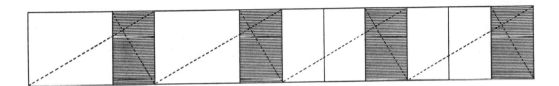

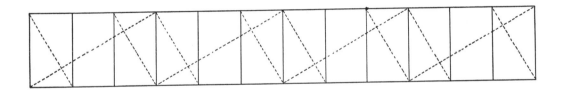

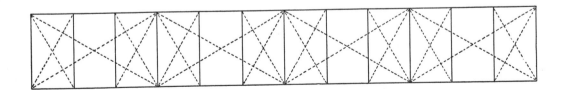

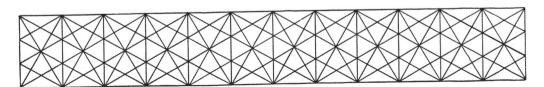

PLATE I

No. 1. Root-three rectangles divided by their diagonals; alternate spaces filled by contrasting colors. The dividing lines of the units are eliminated with the consequent appearance of the diamond units. Each diamond has the ratio of one to the square root of three or 1 to 1.732.

No. 2. Similar to No. 1, but with the addition of the diagonals of the reciprocals lying between each two units.

No. 3. Two reciprocals with one diagonal in each and reversed. By the suppression of the vertical divisions between the reciprocals we obtain a succession of equilateral triangles of contrasting colors.

No. 4. Succession of root-three reciprocals, in each of which is drawn its major diagonals. By the elimination of the vertical divisions between the units we have a succession of root-three diamonds side by side.

No. 5. This is the reverse of No. 3, as the black triangles are at the bottom. The white triangles are divided into four smaller triangles, with the center one of contrasting color.

No. 6. Divide each reciprocal into three parts by drawing lines through the eyes of the long and short diagonals. This gives us a narrow band at top and bottom, and a band of twice the area in the center. Each reciprocal is divided by one long diagonal into two areas of contrasting color and is joined to a similar reciprocal reversed, without the dividing lines. The bands at top and bottom of each reciprocal unit are divided into small triangles and the areas filled in, in contrasting colors; the apexes of the black triangles touching the eyes at the top and the apexes of the white touching the eyes at the bottom of the unit.

PLATE II

ROOT-THREE RECTANGLE — PLATE III

No. 1. The construction of this design is the same as that of diagram No. 5 of Plate I. The diagonals of the root-three unit are omitted, and the diagonals of the two exterior reciprocals only are drawn, with the alternate spaces filled with contrasting colors. (Many of these designs, in which the equilateral triangle and regular hexagon are used as units of pattern, are very familiar, and are used merely to show that they are logically an outgrowth of the dynamic system of symmetry, although the dynamic aspect of their construction has not, previous to Mr. Hambidge, been recognized.)

No. 2. An amplification of No. 1. The hexagons are here divided by connecting the sides, which gives three root-three rectangles crossing one another, and also two equilateral triangles, forming a six-pointed star, with a hexagon in the center. The six pointed star is known as the Seal of Solomon and has been in use from ancient times. The last unit of the band shows still further subdivisions; this process of subdivision may be continued to infinity.

No. 3. If you will refer again to No. 5, Plate I, you will see how this design is constructed. In this case, however, the root-three units encroach upon each other to the extent of one reciprocal, and two diagonals are added to the reciprocal in the center of the unit.

No. 4. Here the units of the pattern are root-three reciprocals, each with two diagonals drawn in, and the alternate spaces filled in, in contrasting colors. Each unit is reversed both in color and in construction. The complete triangles in the design are in the geometrical progression of one to the square root of three in line, and of one to four in area.

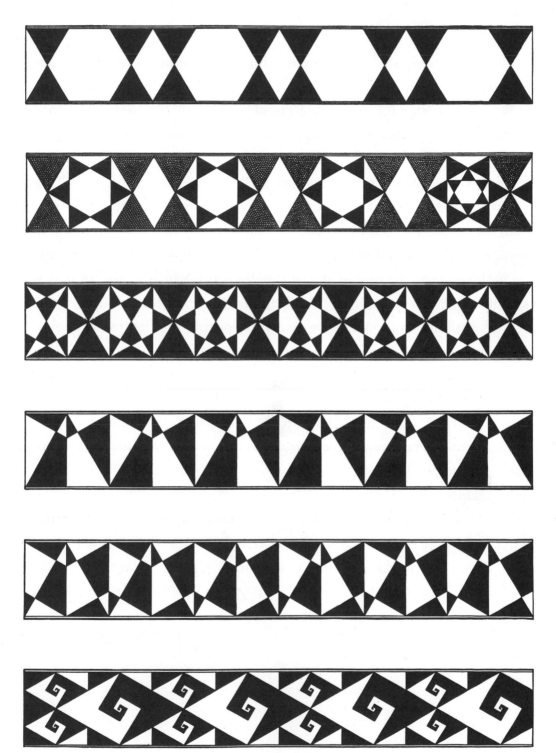

PLATE III

No. 5. The same as No. 4, except for the addition of another diagonal to the units.

No. 6. The angular root-three spiral is used in this design in conjunction with equilateral triangles and root-three rectangles. The construction is difficult to describe, but is quite obvious on inspection. The root-three units are first divided by their long diagonals, resulting in a succession of root-three diamonds each composed of two equilateral triangles. From the center of each diamond are drawn two root-three angular spirals, rotated at an angle of 180° to each other, and terminating at the ends of the minor axis of the diamond, which is also the common base line of two equilateral triangles. On filling the opposite areas with contrasting color, we have two interlocking equilateral triangles. Four similar interlocking units, one quarter of the area of the larger units, are drawn in the triangular areas between each large diamond, and each remaining triangular area is divided into two parts. The area of each vertical division of the pattern is one-half of a root-three rectangle, or two small root-three rectangles one above the other. Observe that all diagonals are parallel to those of the parent rectangles or those of the reciprocals.

A plate of examples of Greek detail is shown opposite. These ornaments have been redrawn from *Examples of Greek and Pompeian Decorative Work*, measured and drawn by James Cromar Watt, and published by B. T. Batsford in London in 1897, long before Mr. Hambidge had formulated his theory of Dynamic Symmetry.

The analysis of these designs, indicated by dotted lines, is by the author.

No. 1. Ornament in White Marble from the Erechtheion, Athens. A Theme in Root-three. (Plate 7, Cromar Watt.)

No. 2. Ornament in White Marble from Athens, Freely Designed within the Limits of a 1.618 Rectangle. (Plate 10, Cromar Watt.)

No. 3. Ormament in White Marble from Lykosoura. A Theme in Root-five. (Plate 8, Cromar Watt.)

Plate III a

Root-three Rectangle — Plate IV

No. 1. Dynamarhythmic fret composed of two root-three angular spirals rotated from the pole, at the intersection of the diagonal of the root-three unit, with the diagonal of the center reciprocal. The black areas are twice the width of the white areas. The units of the design encroach upon each other to the extent of the separating band.

No. 2. In this design the spirals are reversed upon themselves. The black bands are of the same width as the white, and are all in the geometrical progression of one to the square root of three. The black area between each unit is common to two adjoining spirals.

No. 3. Here we have double black and white spirals of similar width forming a continuous fret. The poles of the four spirals are in each instance at the diagonally opposite angles of a root-three rectangle, the long sides of which coincide with the long diagonal of a root-three unit.

No. 4. The units at the top of this design are composed of a root-three rectangle plus its reciprocal, or an area composed of four reciprocals. The spirals which grow from the poles of the end reciprocals are reversed in the center of this area. This admits of the interlocking of the top band with a similar reversed band at the bottom, to the extent of one-third of the area of the reciprocals.

No. 5. Similar in idea to No. 4. The units in this case, composed as above of four root-three reciprocals, are, however, perpendicular to the base of the band, and are interlocked so that the small reciprocals, which are one-third of the area of the larger reciprocals, come tangent end to end.

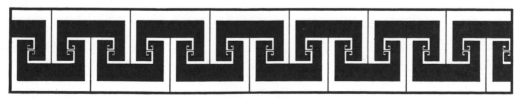

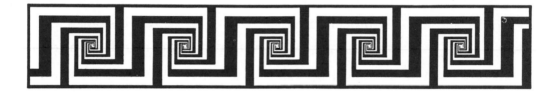

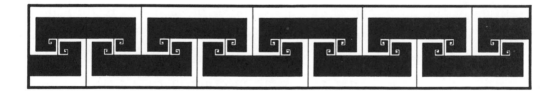

PLATE IV

Root-three Rectangle — Plate V

No. 1. Interlocking s-shaped angular spiral units forming a counter-change pattern. Each unit is a root-three rectangle divided into its reciprocals; from the centers of the reciprocals at the end of each rectangle are rotated two angular spirals at an angle of 180° to each other. The inner spiral of one end reciprocal meeting the outer spiral of the other end reciprocal forming the complete unit.

No. 2. In this design the rectangle is divided into its three reciprocals. In the end reciprocals are placed angular spiral c-shaped units, which are formed by drawing two reversed angular spirals from opposite poles. The center reciprocal is treated in a manner similar to the parent rectangle and the process continued as far as is practical.

No. 3. To construct this design the root-three rectangle is divided into three reciprocals, and the long diagonals drawn in each. From the centers of the inner halves of the diagonals of each end reciprocal are drawn two angular spirals at an angle of 180° to each other, the one meeting the outer edge of the rectangle and the other continued along the diagonal of the center reciprocal, meeting in each case the opposite spiral and forming the angular s-shaped units which together form the letter x. Only the center line of the spiral coincides with the structural lines of the rectangle and of its reciprocals; the width of the bands may be varied as the occasion may demand.

No. 4. In the reciprocal of the rectangle is drawn a long diagonal and two short ones; from the poles at the intersections of the diagonals are drawn two spirals meeting in the center of the reciprocal, and form-

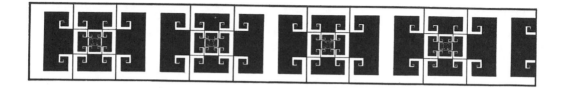

PLATE V

ing an s; from this s, and tangent to it, are drawn reversed segments of the spiral to the corners of the rectangles, and of the reciprocals as far as practical. The angular spirals of the reciprocals are then drawn, and also angular spirals from the same poles, terminating at the corners of the rectangle. The design is then reversed and the triangular areas, as well as the background in the reciprocals of the units filled in with black or color.

No. 5. From two diagonally opposite poles of the reciprocal are drawn two spirals meeting in the center of the reciprocal, and two additional spirals coming tangent to the sides of the reciprocal and continued to meet the opposite curve; one of the resultant areas is filled in with black, and the contrasting area left white. This design is then reversed while behind it, and coinciding with the diagonals of the reversed reciprocals, is drawn an equilateral triangle, forming the completed unit. When this is continued, we have a counterchange design formed of black lotuses with a background of black pyramids, contrasted with white lotuses with a background of white pyramids. It is curious that these concrete forms are purely the result of the structure.

No. 6. From a pole in the center of the unit are drawn four spirals to the sides of the band, and continued to meet the opposite sides; four shorter spirals are drawn meeting a center axis drawn through the pole. From the terminations of the four longer spirals are drawn the diagonals of four root-three rectangles, on which are constructed angular spirals, which are in turn bound together by smaller angular spirals at an angle of 180° and meeting on the axis of the band.

Root-three Rectangle — Plate VI

No. 1. The correct spiral for making this design is that of the 1.775 rectangle, but in order to avoid a separate classification, the root-three spiral is used for the purpose; the difference is 43/1000 of the length of the rectangle. Referring to the description of Fig. 12 in this chapter, we see that the smaller curves interlace with the larger ones, instead of becoming tangent as they do in this design. The axis on which the half-unit is reversed is moved somewhat beyond the point of tangency with the escribed rectangle, leaving a slight gap in the curve, which has to be filled in.

No. 2. A reference to the description of Fig. 13 in this chapter, will show how this design is made with the root-three spiral. The correct spiral is that of the 1.775 rectangle.

No. 3. S-shaped units composed of two root-three spirals, interlacing with similar units in such a way that each s is crossed twice by similar curves, the terminations interlacing and becoming tangent with the sides of the s-curves, in the triangular areas between the crossed s-units. If the poles of the spirals are moved closer to the longitudinal axis of the design, the spiral bands become thinner, and the angle of inclination of the s-units with the top or base line of the design becomes less. The reverse is true if the poles are moved further away from the axis. Many other combinations of the s-curves of various rectangles are possible, but the limitations of this book do not permit of their being shown.

No. 4. Alternating curved and rectangular root-three spirals rotated at an angle of 180° from the longitudinal axis of the design. The distance from pole to pole of the curved spirals, or of the rectangular spirals is determined by the long diagonal of a root-three rectangle, which establishes the axes of the repeats. The outer lines of the band are arbitrary.

No. 5. This design is composed of two wave designs running in opposite directions and in contact with each other. Each wave design is composed of a succession of root-three s-curves, each two successive curves rotated at an angle of 180° from a common pole. The background is filled with free foliation, Greek in character.

PLATE VI

Root-three Rectangle — Plate VII

This surface pattern is designed on a net-work composed of regular hexagons joined together on their angles, leaving an equilateral triangle between each three hexagons. From the poles placed in each of the angles of the hexagons, are rotated two root-three spirals, which meet similar spirals in the center of the hexagon, rotated from poles in the opposite angles of the hexagon, and forming three s-curves crossing each other. Two supplementary spirals are drawn from each pole and joined together forming a curved hexagonal form behind the interlaced s-curves.

PLATE VII

Root-three Rectangle — Plate VIII

The net-work on which this design is based is composed of regular hexagons joined on their angles, and intersecting each other in such a way that around the center of each hexagon are grouped three other hexagons of the same size, the whole forming a web of equilateral triangles. Intersecting each other, in each angle of the hexagons, are three root-three s-curves, from the poles of which are rotated larger spirals (the size of which is governed by their coming tangent with similar spirals from the poles of the unit), rotated at an angle of 180° and joining with similar spirals coming from the opposite direction, and forming three s-curves grouped around an equilateral triangle. Smaller equilateral triangles are placed in the centers of the larger triangles for contrast. The eye carries the lines of the triangles through the design, giving it strong structural quality.

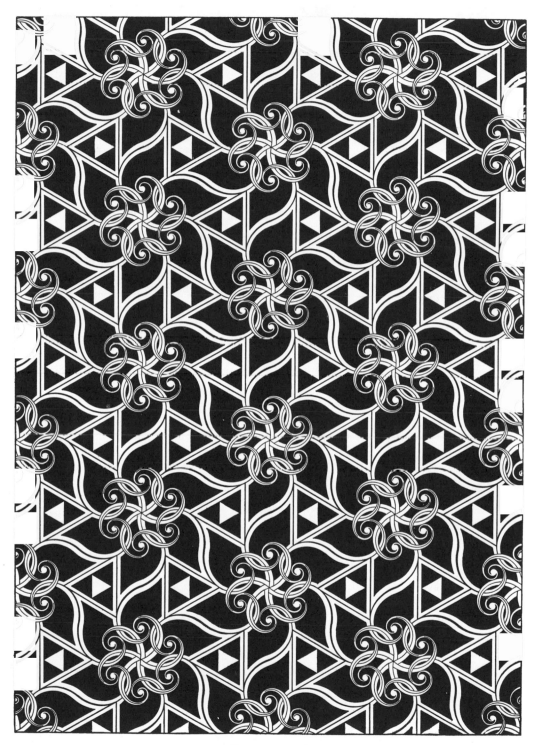

PLATE VIII

Root-three Rectangle — Plate IX

To construct this pattern, a root-three rectangle is divided by its long diagonal, which is crossed at right angles by the diagonals of the two end reciprocals. At the intersections of the diagonals are placed diagonally opposite poles, from which are drawn rectangular spirals joined together by a diagonal band through the rectangle. The z-shaped unit thus formed is then reversed face to face, and again reversed end to end, so that the end reciprocals mutually fit into the center reciprocals of the opposing units. The completed units are then grouped in a square, the repetition of which forms the design.

PLATE IX

CHAPTER X

THE ROOT-FOUR RECTANGLE

The root-four rectangle is the first of the root rectangles whose end is commensurable with its side, being simply in the ratio of 1 to 2, or in area two squares. Its construction is simple. In Fig. 1 on AB, the unit side of the rectangle, describe the square ABCD; with D as center

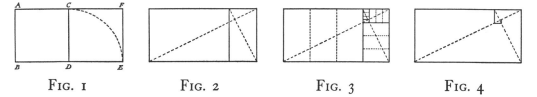

FIG. 1   FIG. 2   FIG. 3   FIG. 4

and DC as radius, describe the quadrant CE meeting BD produced to E; complete the rectangle by producing AC to F and drawing FE. Fig. 2 shows the rectangle divided dynamically by a perpendicular to its diagonal, cutting off the reciprocal which is exactly ¼ the area of the parent rectangle. The square on the side is four times the area of the square on the end. The progression of gnomons around the pole is shown in Fig. 3; each gnomon is composed of three root-four rectangles. The angular spiral is shown in Fig. 4.

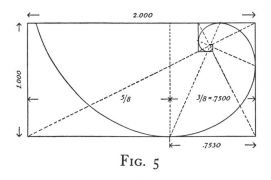

FIG. 5

The spiral of the root-four rectangle comes tangent with the side of the rectangle at a point .7530 distant from the right side of the diagram shown in Fig. 5. The author has established the point at approximately ⅜ or .750 distant from the end of the rectangle; the discrepancy is 3/1000 of the length and is scarcely perceptible. For practical purposes it is easier to measure ⅜ of the length, as the point can be established in a rectangle of any size with a pair of dividers.

Fig. 6 shows the spiral reversed on the approximate point of tangency, with the two spirals rotated at an angle of 180°. This is the unit of the continuous band, which repeats on the axes indicated by the dotted lines. The doubly reversed unit is shown in Fig. 7 with the axes also indicated on which the figure may be repeated.

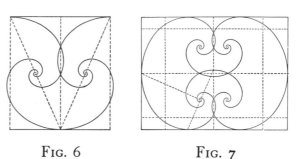

FIG. 6   FIG. 7

In Fig. 8 we approach a matter which seems to be, as far as the author is aware, new to geometry. If true, it establishes a relation-

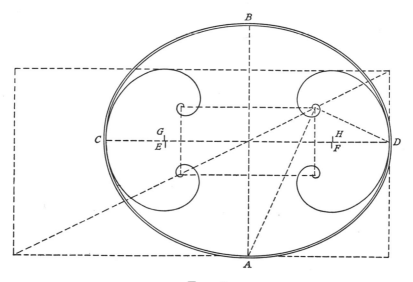

FIG. 8

ship between the logarithmic spiral and the true ellipse, which is one of the conic sections. The inference is obvious. One mathematician to whom the author has spoken of the matter says that it is impossible that it can be true, for the reason that an ellipse has two foci, while the logarithmic spiral, on the contrary, has only one pole; but for purposes of argument, let us examine the diagram, which is constructed as follows: We draw a root-four rectangle as in Fig. 5, and draw its spiral; which is reversed on the axis AB, as in Fig. 8, established by the point of tangency with the side of the rectangle, and the resultant figure is again reversed on the axis CD, established by the point of tangency of the spiral with the end of the rectangle. When this figure is complete, the resultant ellipse is composed of four quadrant segments of the spiral, each segment lying between two radii vectors at right angles to each other. The four poles from which the spirals are drawn lie in the corners of a smaller root-four rectangle. The second ellipse, exterior to the first, has been drawn with an ellipsograph in order to show by comparison that the ellipse composed of the quadrant segments of the spiral is identical with that drawn with the ellipsograph. This could not be shown otherwise, as the paths travelled by both are the same, and show as one line. The two foci of the inner ellipse are indicated at E and F. The foci of the outer ellipse are a little further from the center at the points G and H.

The author has tested this method with the spirals of many rectangles, and the results have always been the same. The four foci from which the spirals are drawn always lie in the corners of a rectangle similar to that which determines the spiral.

The method of finding the foci of any ellipse is shown in Fig. 9. Let AB and CD, which cross each other at right angles, represent the transverse and conjugate diameters of the ellipse. Parallel to AB draw EF and GH, through C and D; and parallel to CD draw EG and FH, through A and B, completing the rectangle. With D as a center and DG or DH as a radius, describe the semicircle GIJH, cutting the transverse diameter AB at I and J, which are the foci. By placing pins at the points I, C, and J, and stretching a linen thread around them, and then removing

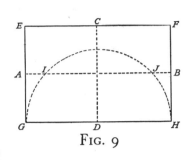

Fig. 9

the pin at C, a true ellipse may be drawn, allowing of course for inequalities resulting from unequal stretching of the thread.

CHAPTER XI

ROOT-FOUR RECTANGLE — PLATES AND DESCRIPTIONS

PLATE I

No. 1. The upper part is composed of a series of root-four rectangles from the opposite poles of which are drawn angular spirals, meeting in the center of the rectangle. Additional angular spirals are rotated from the same poles, also meeting in the centers of the rectangles, at a point somewhat more than one-half of the height, which allows for the thickness of the lines separating the rectangles. The lower part of the design is similar to the upper part, but reversed, and interlocked to the extent of one-third of the height of the entire design, and the background filled in with black. From the lines dividing the rectangles of the upper and lower parts are drawn supplementary root-four s-curves, which are joined to the sides of the band by smaller s-curves. The black bands at top and bottom of the band are in a root-four ratio.

No. 2. A series of interlacing root-four reversed spiral curves at the top of the band, interlacing with and tangent to a similar succession of reversed spiral curves at the bottom, supplemented with free ornament.

No. 3. Freely interlaced s-shaped root-four spirals, elaborated by the addition of free ornament of a Renaissance character.

No. 4. Reversed root-four spirals are rotated at an angle of 180° from poles on an axis through the center of the band, forming a continuous design. Supplementary spirals are rotated from the same poles to the sides of the band terminating in small free spirals. The structural bands are then elaborated with free ornament in rhythm with the spirals.

PLATE I

Root-four Rectangle — Plate II

From the center and from each of the corners of a square are rotated four root-four angular spirals, meeting and joining with similar spirals from the center and corners of the adjoining squares, forming an all-over pattern. Observe that parts of the spirals of one square encroach upon the adjoining square and form part of a continuous succession of angular s-shaped units, which are crossed at right angles with a similar succession of units.

PLATE II

Root-four Rectangle — Plate III

From the four poles of two root-four angular s-shaped units crossed at right angles, are rotated at an angle of 180° four root-four curved spirals of similar thickness, increasing proportionately to the points where they join similar spirals from the opposite direction, the whole forming an all-over pattern of angular s-shapes, alternating with curved s-shapes, crossed at right angles with similar angular s-shapes alternating with curved s-shapes.

PLATE III

CHAPTER XII

THE ROOT-FIVE RECTANGLE

Geometry is supposed to have been introduced into Greece by Thales, but to Pythagoras, who was an extensive traveler, and according to Callimachus derived much of his mathematical knowledge from Egypt, is due the credit for having raised it to the rank of an exact science. Eudemus ascribes to Pythagoras the construction of the regular solids which to the Greeks represented the five elements of their cosmology: fire (tetrahedron), earth (cube), air (octahedron), universe or ether (dodecahedron), water (icosahedron). Pythagoras and his school also developed the principles of proportion with which the present chapter is especially concerned.

To construct a root-five rectangle we first draw a square, Fig. 1, and bisect the side AC at E; with EB or ED as a radius describe the semicircle GBDH meeting the side of the square AC extended at G and H; by extending the side BD of the square to I and J, and drawing IG and JH, we complete the rectangle. This method of construction is based on that of Prop. 11, Book II of Euclid, already described for the construction of the whirling square rectangle; the resultant figure is a compound shape composed of a square in the center and a small whirling square rectangle, or a reciprocal, on each end, or a whirling square rectangle plus its reciprocal. Assuming the square to be unity, we have: $1.000 + .618 + .618 = 2.236$ or the square root of five. This

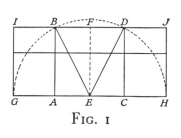

FIG. 1

shape was a favorite one with the Greeks, who used it in various combinations with the square, and the 1.618 rectangle, as the basis of construction of many beautiful designs. The ground plan of the Parthenon
was, according to the analysis of Mr. Hambidge, a square and a root-
five rectangle, plus the reciprocal of this figure, also a square and a
root-five rectangle.[1] As a balanced compound shape in which the ratio
of extreme and mean proportion is inherent, it is of great value for
purposes of design.

Fig. 2 shows the root-five rectangle as a simple form, and divided
in a similar way to the other root-rectangles. Its reciprocal is 1/5 of the

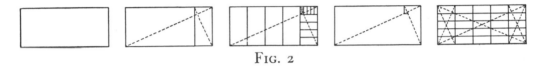

FIG. 2

area, and the gnomon is composed of four reciprocals. As a simple
shape, the author has not found it very prolific for purposes of Dynamarhythmic Design, as the contrast in length of end to side of the rectangle
seems to be too great, and the angular spiral diminishes or increases
too rapidly for practical use. The spiral however is very graceful, and
may be used to great advantage where attenuated forms are required,
in ironwork, for example.

The construction of the pentagram or pentacle, in which the ratio
of extreme and mean proportion is inherent, was discovered by the
Pythagoreans in the Sixth Century B.C. and was used by them as the
symbol of health, and as the seal of their school. The pentagram, as
well as the root-five rectangle, may be constructed by an amplification
of Prop. 11, Book II of Euclid, as in Fig. 3. Let AB be the base of
the pentagram and on AB describe the square ABCD, and bisect AB at E.

[1] *The Parthenon and Other Greek Temples*, by Jay Hambidge (New Haven, Yale University Press, 1924).

With ED or EC as a radius describe the semicircle FCDG meeting AB

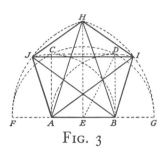

FIG. 3

produced to F and G. Erect the perpendicular EH and with AG as a radius describe the arc GH. With BF as a radius describe the arc FH, connect BH and AH. With BA as a radius describe the arc ADI, and with AB as a radius describe the arc BCJ. Join JI, JB, HA, HB and AI, and the pentagram is complete. Join AJHIB and we have the completed pentagon. The isosceles triangle ABC, Fig. 4, was from remote antiquity the basis of many interesting geometrical constructions. The smaller triangle ABD is the reciprocal of ABC, and the remaining triangle BDC is the gnomon. At D, the side AC of the triangle ABC is cut in extreme and mean proportion. The reciprocal in each instance may be divided into a smaller reciprocal and a gno-mon, and the process may be continued to infinity. The pentagram and its escribed pentagon may be drawn with one continuous line.

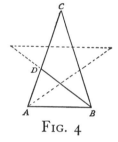

FIG. 4

The point where the spiral of the root-five rectangle comes tangent with the side is .7996 distant from the right side of the diagram, Fig. 5, which is approximately 4/11 of the length; 4/11 of 2.236 = .8131,

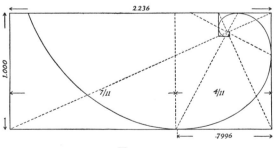

FIG. 5

therefore the difference is about 135/10000 of the length of the rectangle. For purposes of de-sign 4/11 is sufficiently ac-curate.

In Fig. 6, the spiral is re-versed on the approximate point of tangency, and from each pole is rotated a similar spiral at an angle of 180°. This unit, when repeated on the axes indicated, forms a continuous band.

Fig. 7 shows the doubly reversed unit, which may be repeated end to end, or side to side, on the axes. A surface pattern may be made by re-

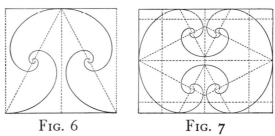

Fig. 6   Fig. 7

peating in both directions. The s-shaped curve is constructed in the same way as that of the root-two rectangle, and the wave pattern in a like manner to those of the other rectangles.

CHAPTER XIII

ROOT-FIVE RECTANGLE — PLATES AND DESCRIPTIONS

PLATE I

No. 1. All-over pattern constructed by crossing two root-five rectangles, with their diagonals and diagonals of their reciprocals, at right angles. One-half of each end reciprocal is eliminated, so that the unit of the repeat is a square composed of four-fifths of each of the two crossed root-five rectangles. The diagonals of the reciprocals are carried through to the sides of the square, and the dividing lines of only the two crossed center reciprocals are retained. The alternate areas are filled in, in tone or color.

No. 2. Pentagonal unit composed of isosceles triangles, each of which is formed of a succession of like triangles in a continued ratio, forming in each case a triangular spiral. The inner pentagon is likewise divided. The process may be continued to infinity.

No. 3. To construct this unit a circle is drawn around a pentagon within which are drawn its diagonals resulting in the smaller related pentagon in the center. From the poles located in the angles of the smaller pentagon are drawn five root-five spirals to the angles of the larger pentagon. From the same poles are drawn supplementary spirals interlacing with the adjoining spirals and then reversed and continued to a common pole in the center of the unit.

No. 4. Somewhat similar design to No. 3 except that in this case the supplementary spirals are continued to a point where they abut the adjoining supplementary spirals.

PLATE I

No. 1. Double interlacing wave pattern of root-five s-curves, all drawn from poles lying on the horizontal axis in the center of the band. The thickness of the s-curves is regulated by the distance between the poles and the small ends of the spirals generated therefrom; if the s-curves were of less thickness the poles would be relatively further apart and the spirals would not touch. This would result in a design of similar character but of a somewhat different appearance.

No. 2. Double row of alternating black on white, and white on black root-five s-curves. The unit of this design is constructed by dividing a root-five rectangle into its reciprocals, and dividing one reciprocal in a like manner. From a pole in the center of this reciprocal, angular spirals are drawn in opposite directions, meeting similar angular spirals drawn from poles in the center of every fourth reciprocal. From the same poles are then drawn the curved spirals tangent to the sides of the rectangles.

No. 3. Attenuated root-five s-curves interlaced so that the poles lie in the angles produced by the crossing of the curves. The construction is supplemented by the addition of foliated spirals in rhythm with the design.

No. 4. The unit of this design fills two reciprocals of a root-five rectangle. The pole lies in the center of this area and from it are revolved in two directions root-five spirals coming tangent with the sides and continued in a straight line to the corners. Additional spirals are drawn on both sides giving the requisite thickness and this con-

PLATE II

struction is then supplemented by the addition of spirals terminating in foliated ornament of a Gothic character.

No. 5. This design is based on a wave pattern of root-five s-curves drawn from poles lying on a horizontal axis. From the same poles four additional root-five spirals are drawn, each pair crossing and terminating in small volutes. Free foliated ornament is then added in rhythm with the spirals.

CHAPTER XIV

THE 1.5388 AND 2.09 RECTANGLES

The small bronze ornament mentioned in the Foreword, which suggested to the author the idea of using the logarithmic spirals of various ratios for purposes of design, can be constructed correctly in but one rectangle, that is the rectangle which is entirely filled by the curve. The points of tangency with the sides A, B, C, D, E, F, etc., are exactly on the lines which define the reciprocals of the rectangle. The ratio is

1 to 1.5388, Fig. 1. Each quadrant segment of the spiral entirely fills the successive gnomons. The reversed curve is shown in Fig. 2, and exactly

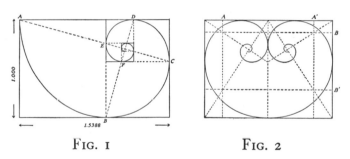

FIG. 1   FIG. 2

fills two reciprocals of the rectangle shown in Fig. 1. The unit may be expanded into a band by repeating on the axes A, A', B, B', indicated by the dotted lines.

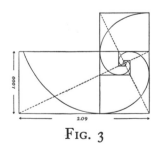

FIG. 3

The spiral of the 2.09 rectangle has the unique property of coming tangent with the side of the rectangle at a point just twice the distance of the pole from the right end of the rectangle, Fig. 3. When the spiral is rotated from the pole at an angle of 180°, the double curve occupies a rectangle of the same shape as the parent rectangle, but in this case the pole is in the center and the two curves exactly fill the space. When this unit is reversed on the sides of the rectangle, it

forms a running band in which the spiral curves are exactly tangent. In Fig. 4 the spiral is once reversed on the axis defined by the point of tangency with the side of the rectangle, and again on an axis which coincides with the upper side of the 2.09 rectangle from which the curve is generated; this results in the appearance of reciprocal reversed spiral areas when

Fig. 4

the spirals are rotated at an angle of 180° from the poles.

CHAPTER XV

1.5388 AND 2.09 RECTANGLES — PLATE AND DESCRIPTIONS

No. 1. To construct the unit of this band an angular spiral is drawn, completely filling a 1.5388 rectangle. The width of the spiral should be narrow enough to admit of a background of considerable contrast. A similar spiral is then drawn and turned so that the open ends come together in such a way that each lies against the closed ends of the spirals of the opposite reciprocals. The open ends of the spirals are then completed by continuing the bands to the poles of the opposite rectangle. This band may be made into an all-over pattern.

No. 2. Continuous wave pattern formed of a succession of 1.5388 s-curves drawn from poles lying on a horizontal axis, intersecting and interlacing with a similar pattern running in the opposite direction.

No. 3. The simple and logical design formed by reversing the 2.09 spiral on the point of tangency with the rectangle, and then rotating similar spirals at an angle of 180° from the same poles and continuing the process to any desired length. The 2.09 rectangle is the only rectangle in which the spirals become tangent on the axis of the repeat. In rectangles less than 2.09 the spirals intersect each other on the axis of the repeat, and in rectangles greater than 2.09 the reversed spiral forms do not touch each other on the axis of the repeat. This design may be formed into an all-over pattern.

No. 4. The unit constructed of 2.09 spirals as described in Fig. 4, interlacing with similar units on the perpendicular axes.

No. 5. To construct this design, a reversed 2.09 spiral is drawn and from the poles similar spirals are revolved at an angle of 180° ending at points coinciding with the sides of the rectangle which defines the space enclosing the reversed spiral; the spirals are then continued in the form of s-curves which interlace with the similar curves of the adjoining units. Between each two units are drawn smaller crossed s-curves and the entire design reversed on the horizontal axis. The addition of foliated ornament completes the design.

PLATE I

CHAPTER XVI

ON THE LAYOUT OF BOOK PAGES

In conclusion the author wishes to describe his method of layout for book pages. The root-two rectangle is an ideal shape for the purpose, as the shape is the same when the book is open as it is when closed. The annexed diagram, Fig. 1, will make this clear. Let AB represent the

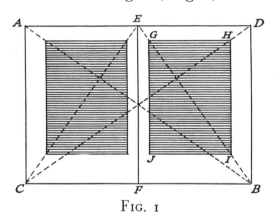

FIG. 1

open book, which in this case is a root-two rectangle. When the diagonals AB and CD have been drawn and crossed at right angles with the diagonals of the reciprocals CE and BE, and the center line FE is drawn, we mark the width of the type page GH, upon the diagonals CD and BE. Then by drawing HI intersecting again the diagonal BE, and IJ, we complete the rectangle of the type page, which is now the same as the book page, and in consequent harmony with it. The process is repeated for the opposite page. Our margins are now in a continued ratio of 1 to 1.4142, and the two inner margins are equal to one outer margin. The size of the type page depends largely upon the character of the book. Small type as a rule requires small margins, and large type looks better with larger margins. The author has found that one half, or the reciprocal of the book page, makes an excellent type page for most purposes. The present volume is laid out upon the above principles. An allowance of course should be made for the binding. If the book lies flat when open this is unnecessary. Considerable good judgment is required, as a good lay-out may easily be spoiled by poor binding or trimming of the page.

For other shapes, Fig. 2, the same principle is used of crossing the diagonal of the open book with the diagonal of a single page. It will be observed, however, that these diagonals are not at right angles to each other, as they are in the root-two layout, and that the margins

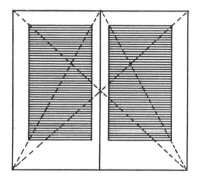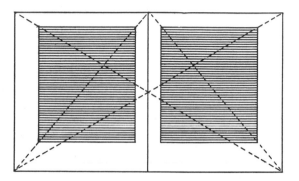

FIG. 2

are not in a continued ratio. The inner margin bears the same relation-ship to the top margin, however, as the outer margin bears to the lower. The two inner margins are equal to one outer, and the type page is the same as the book page. It is interesting to observe that when the diag-onal of the entire rectangle is crossed with the diagonal of its half, it cuts the figure, on the intersection of the two diagonals, into exactly three parts.

A scale of ratios may be constructed in any of the above figures, similar to those shown in the root rectangles, which will be found very useful for the proportioning of headbands and other decorations. If illustrations are used, their shapes should conform if possible to the shape of the open book or to that of the book page.

APPENDIX

LOCATION OF THE POINT OF CONTACT OF THE LOGARITHMIC SPIRAL INSCRIBED IN A ROOT RECTANGLE WITH THE LONGER SIDE

To obtain a general solution of this problem, we assume a rectangle with sides in the ratio $I : p$ and call d the distance from the vertex of the rectangle to the point of contact.

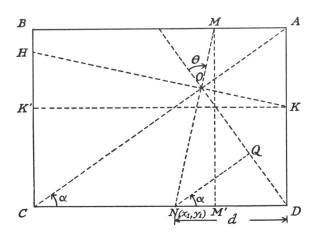

We first find

THE EQUATION OF THE SPIRAL.

Assuming this equation in the general form

$$(1) \qquad \rho = e^{a\theta},$$

it will be convenient to take for axes of coördinates the diagonal of the rectangle (y-axis) and the perpendic-ular drawn to it from D (x-axis).

Let M, K, N, H, be four successive points of contact of two sets of mutually perpendicular tangents to the spiral. Then we know from the equation of the spiral that the lines MN and KH pass through the origin, where they meet at right angles.

We draw MM' and KK' respectively perpendicular to the sides of the rectangle, thus forming the similar triangles $MM'N$ and $KK'H$, from which we have

$$\frac{KH}{MN} = \frac{KK'}{MM'} = p.$$

118

Since

$$MN = OM + ON = e^{a\theta_1} + e^{a(\theta_1 + \pi)} = e^{a\theta_1}(1 + e^{a\pi})$$

and

$$KH = OK + OH = e^{a\left(\theta_1 + \frac{\pi}{2}\right)} + e^{a\left(\theta_1 + \frac{3\pi}{2}\right)} = e^{a\left(\theta_1 + \frac{\pi}{2}\right)}(1 + e^{a\pi}),$$

$$\frac{KH}{MN} = \frac{e^{a\left(\theta_1 + \frac{\pi}{2}\right)}}{e^{a\theta_1}} = e^{\frac{a\pi}{2}},$$

and therefore from

$$e^{\frac{a\pi}{2}} = p$$

follows

$$\frac{a\,\pi}{2} = \log p,$$

or

(2)
$$a = \frac{\log p^2}{\pi},$$

which determines the equation of the spiral.[1]

We now seek an equation containing d, by equating the slope of the side of the rectangle to the general form of the slope of the spiral.

To do this we first find the

COÖRDINATES OF C AND D.

The various right triangles in the figure give the following relations:

$$AC = \sqrt{1 + p^2},$$

$$AO = \frac{\overline{AD}^2}{AC} = \frac{1}{\sqrt{1 + p^2}} \text{ or } \frac{\sqrt{1 + p^2}}{1 + p^2},$$

$$CO = \frac{\overline{CD}^2}{AC} = \frac{p^2}{\sqrt{1 + p^2}} \text{ or } \frac{p^2\sqrt{1 + p^2}}{1 + p^2},$$

$$DO = \sqrt{AO \times CO} = \frac{p\sqrt{1 + p^2}}{1 + p^2}.$$

---

[1] Incidentally this is proof of the fact that, given a rectangle, there is only one spiral of the type $\rho = e^{a\theta}$ inscribed in it.

Therefore the coördinates of C are

$$x = 0, \quad y = -\frac{p^2\sqrt{1+p^2}}{1+p^2}$$

and the coördinates of D are

$$x = -\frac{p\sqrt{1+p^2}}{1+p^2}, \quad y = 0.$$

Then we

EVALUATE x_1 AND y_1 (THE COÖRDINATES OF N) IN TERMS OF d.

From the figure again

$$x_1 = OD - DQ = -\frac{p\sqrt{1+p^2}}{1+p^2} + d\sin\alpha = -\frac{p\sqrt{1+p^2}}{1+p^2} + d\frac{\sqrt{1+p^2}}{1+p^2}$$

$$= (d-p)\frac{\sqrt{1+p^2}}{1+p^2},$$

$$y_1 = QN = d\cos\alpha = -\frac{dp\sqrt{1+p^2}}{1+p^2}.$$

Using the general form

(3) $$y = mx + b$$

of the equation of a straight line, we find for the line CD, making use of the fact that it passes through C and D,

$$b = -\frac{p^2\sqrt{1+p^2}}{1+p^2}$$

and

$$0 = -m\frac{p\sqrt{1+p^2}}{1+p^2} - \frac{p^2\sqrt{1+p^2}}{1+p^2}$$

or the slope of CD is

(4) $$m = -p.$$

We now obtain the general form of the

SLOPE OF THE SPIRAL $\rho = e^{a\theta}$.

Transforming to cartesian coördinates by means of the relations

(5) $$\rho = \sqrt{x^2 + y^2}, \quad \tan\theta = \frac{y}{x},$$

(6) $$x^2 + y^2 = e^{2a\tan^{-1}\frac{y}{x}}.$$

Differentiating,

$$2x + 2y\frac{dy}{dx} = e^{2a\,\tan^{-1}\frac{y}{x}} \cdot 2a\,\frac{x\dfrac{dy}{dx} - y}{x^2 + y^2},$$

and using (6) to simplify this, we find

$$x + y\frac{dy}{dx} = ax\frac{dy}{dx} - ay,$$

whence the slope of the spiral is given by the formula

(7)
$$\frac{dy}{dx} = \frac{ay + x}{ax - y}.$$

We are now in a position to obtain an
EQUATION CONNECTING a AND d.

We have at the point N (the slope of CD must be the same as that of the spiral),

$$\frac{ay + x}{ax - y} = -p.$$

Substituting in this the values found above for x_1 and y_1, in terms of d

$$\frac{-\dfrac{ad\,p\sqrt{1 + p^2}}{1 + p^2} + (d - p)\dfrac{\sqrt{1 + p^2}}{1 + p^2}}{a(d - p)\dfrac{\sqrt{1 + p^2}}{1 + p^2} + \dfrac{dp\sqrt{1 + p^2}}{1 + p^2}} = -p,$$

which becomes after simplification

$$d - p - adp = -ap(d - p) - dp^2,$$

and solving for d we find

(8)
$$d = \frac{p(1 + ap)}{1 + p^2}.$$

Substituting in this the value found at the beginning for a we have the following formula for d,

(9)
$$d = \frac{p(\pi + p\log p^2)}{\pi(1 + p^2)} \quad \text{or} \quad \frac{p}{1 + p^2} + \frac{p^2\log p^2}{\pi(1 + p^2)}.$$

We finally obtain the actual numerical results by putting in this formula the various values of p:

1    $p = \sqrt{2}$

$$d = \frac{1.4142}{3} + \frac{2 \times .6931 \times .3183}{3} = \frac{1.8554}{3} = \underline{\underline{.6185}}^{-}$$

2    $p = \sqrt{3}$

$$d = \frac{1.7321}{4} + \frac{3 \times 1.0986 \times .3183}{4} = \frac{2.7812}{4} = \underline{\underline{.6953}}$$

3    $p = \sqrt{4} = 2$

$$d = \frac{2}{5} + \frac{4 \times 1.3863 \times .3183}{5} = \frac{3.7650}{5} \qquad = \underline{\underline{.7530}}$$

4    $p = \sqrt{5}$

$$d = \frac{2.2361}{6} + \frac{5 \times 1.6094 \times .3183}{6} = \frac{4.7975}{6} = \underline{\underline{.7996}}^{-}$$

5    $p = \frac{1 + \sqrt{5}}{2} = 1.6181$

$$d = .4472 + (.7236 \times .9624 \times .3183) \qquad = \underline{\underline{.6687}}^{-}$$

If the short side of the rectangle is 10 cms., it suffices to multiply these results by 10 to obtain the value of d in cms.

R. ALBRECHT CARRIÉ.

A CATALOGUE OF SELECTED DOVER BOOKS
IN ALL FIELDS OF INTEREST

A CATALOGUE OF SELECTED DOVER BOOKS
IN ALL FIELDS OF INTEREST

LEATHER TOOLING AND CARVING, Chris H. Groneman. One of few books concentrating on tooling and carving, with complete instructions and grid designs for 39 projects ranging from bookmarks to bags. 148 illustrations. 111pp. 7⅞ x 10.
23061-9 Pa. $2.50

THE CODEX NUTTALL, A PICTURE MANUSCRIPT FROM ANCIENT MEXICO, as first edited by Zelia Nuttall. Only inexpensive edition, in full color, of a pre-Columbian Mexican (Mixtec) book. 88 color plates show kings, gods, heroes, temples, sacrifices. New explanatory, historical introduction by Arthur G. Miller. 96pp. 11⅜ x 8½.
23168-2 Pa. $7.50

AMERICAN PRIMITIVE PAINTING, Jean Lipman. Classic collection of an enduring American tradition. 109 plates, 8 in full color—portraits, landscapes, Biblical and historical scenes, etc., showing family groups, farm life, and so on. 80pp. of lucid text. 8⅜ x 11¼.
22815-0 Pa. $5.00

WILL BRADLEY: HIS GRAPHIC ART, edited by Clarence P. Hornung. Striking collection of work by foremost practitioner of Art Nouveau in America: posters, cover designs, sample pages, advertisements, other illustrations. 97 plates, including 8 in full color and 19 in two colors. 97pp. 9⅜ x 12¼.
20701-3 Pa. $4.00
22120-2 Clothbd. $10.00

AN ATLAS OF ANATOMY FOR ARTISTS, Fritz Schider. Finest text, working book. Full text, plus anatomical illustrations; plates by great artists showing anatomy. 593 illustrations. 192pp. 7⅞ x 10¾.
20241-0 Clothbd. $6.95

THE GIBSON GIRL AND HER AMERICA, Charles Dana Gibson. 155 finest drawings of effervescent world of 1900-1910: the Gibson Girl and her loves, amusements, adventures, Mr. Pipp, etc. Selected by E. Gillon; introduction by Henry Pitz. 144pp. 8¼ x 11⅜.
21986-0 Pa. $3.50

STAINED GLASS CRAFT, J.A.F. Divine, G. Blachford. One of the very few books that tell the beginner exactly what he needs to know: planning cuts, making shapes, avoiding design weaknesses, fitting glass, etc. 93 illustrations. 115pp.
22812-6 Pa. $1.75

AUSTRIAN COOKING AND BAKING, Gretel Beer. Authentic thick soups, wiener schnitzel, veal goulash, more, plus dumplings, puff pastries, nut cakes, sacher tortes, other great Austrian desserts. 224pp.   USO 23220-4 Pa. $2.50

CHEESES OF THE WORLD, U.S.D.A. Dictionary of cheeses containing descriptions of over 400 varieties of cheese from common Cheddar to exotic Surati. Up to two pages are given to important cheeses like Camembert, Cottage, Edam, etc. 151pp.   22831-2 Pa. $1.50

TRITTON'S GUIDE TO BETTER WINE AND BEER MAKING FOR BEGINNERS, S.M. Tritton. All you need to know to make family-sized quantities of over 100 types of grape, fruit, herb, vegetable wines; plus beers, mead, cider, more. 11 illustrations. 157pp.   USO 22528-3 Pa. $2.25

DECORATIVE LABELS FOR HOME CANNING, PRESERVING, AND OTHER HOUSEHOLD AND GIFT USES, Theodore Menten. 128 gummed, perforated labels, beautifully printed in 2 colors. 12 versions in traditional, Art Nouveau, Art Deco styles. Adhere to metal, glass, wood, most plastics. 24pp. 8¼ x 11. 23219-0 Pa. $2.00

FIVE ACRES AND INDEPENDENCE, Maurice G. Kains. Great back-to-the-land classic explains basics of self-sufficient farming: economics, plants, crops, animals, orchards, soils, land selection, host of other necessary things. Do not confuse with skimpy faddist literature; Kains was one of America's greatest agriculturalists. 95 illustrations. 397pp.   20974-1 Pa. $3.00

GROWING VEGETABLES IN THE HOME GARDEN, U.S. Dept. of Agriculture. Basic information on site, soil conditions, selection of vegetables, planting, cultivation, gathering. Up-to-date, concise, authoritative. Covers 60 vegetables. 30 illustrations. 123pp.   23167-4 Pa. $1.35

FRUITS FOR THE HOME GARDEN, Dr. U.P. Hedrick. A chapter covering each type of garden fruit, advice on plant care, soils, grafting, pruning, sprays, transplanting, and much more! Very full. 53 illustrations. 175pp.   22044-0 Pa. $2.50

GARDENING ON SANDY SOIL IN NORTH TEMPERATE AREAS, Christine Kelway. Is your soil too light, too sandy? Improve your soil, select plants that survive under such conditions. Both vegetables and flowers. 42 photos. 148pp.
USO 23199-2 Pa. $2.50

THE FRAGRANT GARDEN: A BOOK ABOUT SWEET SCENTED FLOWERS AND LEAVES, Louise Beebe Wilder. Fullest, best book on growing plants for their fragrances. Descriptions of hundreds of plants, both well-known and overlooked. 407pp.
23071-6 Pa. **$4.00**

EASY GARDENING WITH DROUGHT-RESISTANT PLANTS, Arno and Irene Nehrling. Authoritative guide to gardening with plants that require a minimum of water: seashore, desert, and rock gardens; house plants; annuals and perennials; much more. 190 illustrations. 320pp.   23230-1 Pa. $3.50

THE MAGIC MOVING PICTURE BOOK, Bliss, Sands & Co. The pictures in this book move! Volcanoes erupt, a house burns, a serpentine dancer wiggles her way through a number. By using a specially ruled acetate screen provided, you can obtain these and 15 other startling effects. Originally "The Motograph Moving Picture Book." 32pp. 8¼ x 11.   23224-7 Pa. $1.75

STRING FIGURES AND HOW TO MAKE THEM, Caroline F. Jayne. Fullest, clearest instructions on string figures from around world: Eskimo, Navajo, Lapp, Europe, more. Cats cradle, moving spear, lightning, stars. Introduction by A.C. Haddon. 950 illustrations. 407pp.   20152-X Pa. $3.50

PAPER FOLDING FOR BEGINNERS, William D. Murray and Francis J. Rigney. Clearest book on market for making origami sail boats, roosters, frogs that move legs, cups, bonbon boxes. 40 projects. More than 275 illustrations. Photographs. 94pp.
20713-7 Pa. $1.25

INDIAN SIGN LANGUAGE, William Tomkins. Over 525 signs developed by Sioux, Blackfoot, Cheyenne, Arapahoe and other tribes. Written instructions and diagrams: how to make words, construct sentences. Also 290 pictographs of Sioux and Ojibway tribes. 111pp. 6⅛ x 9¼.   22029-X Pa. $1.50

BOOMERANGS: HOW TO MAKE AND THROW THEM, Bernard S. Mason. Easy to make and throw, dozens of designs: cross-stick, pinwheel, boomabird, tumblestick, Australian curved stick boomerang. Complete throwing instructions. All safe. 99pp.   23028-7 Pa. $1.75

25 KITES THAT FLY, Leslie Hunt. Full, easy to follow instructions for kites made from inexpensive materials. Many novelties. Reeling, raising, designing your own. 70 illustrations. 110pp.   22550-X Pa. $1.25

TRICKS AND GAMES ON THE POOL TABLE, Fred Herrmann. 79 tricks and games, some solitaires, some for 2 or more players, some competitive; mystifying shots and throws, unusual carom, tricks involving cork, coins, a hat, more. 77 figures. 95pp.   21814-7 Pa. $1.25

WOODCRAFT AND CAMPING, Bernard S. Mason. How to make a quick emergency shelter, select woods that will burn immediately, make do with limited supplies, etc. Also making many things out of wood, rawhide, bark, at camp. Formerly titled Woodcraft. 295 illustrations. 580pp.   21951-8 Pa. $4.00

AN INTRODUCTION TO CHESS MOVES AND TACTICS SIMPLY EXPLAINED, Leonard Barden. Informal intermediate introduction: reasons for moves, tactics, openings, traps, positional play, endgame. Isolates patterns. 102pp. USO 21210-6 Pa. $1.35

LASKER'S MANUAL OF CHESS, Dr. Emanuel Lasker. Great world champion offers very thorough coverage of all aspects of chess. Combinations, position play, openings, endgame, aesthetics of chess, philosophy of struggle, much more. Filled with analyzed games. 390pp.   20640-8 Pa. $4.00

EAST O' THE SUN AND WEST O' THE MOON, George W. Dasent. Considered the best of all translations of these Norwegian folk tales, this collection has been enjoyed by generations of children (and folklorists too). Includes True and Untrue, Why the Sea is Salt, East O' the Sun and West O' the Moon, Why the Bear is Stumpy-Tailed, Boots and the Troll, The Cock and the Hen, Rich Peter the Pedlar, and 52 more. The only edition with all 59 tales. 77 illustrations by Erik Werenskiold and Theodor Kittelsen. xv + 418pp. 22521-6 Paperbound **$4.00**

GOOPS AND HOW TO BE THEM, Gelett Burgess. Classic of tongue-in-cheek humor, masquerading as etiquette book. 87 verses, twice as many cartoons, show mischievous Goops as they demonstrate to children virtues of table manners, neatness, courtesy, etc. Favorite for generations. viii + 88pp. $6\frac{1}{2}$ x $9\frac{1}{4}$.
22233-0 Paperbound **$2.00**

ALICE'S ADVENTURES UNDER GROUND, Lewis Carroll. The first version, quite different from the final *Alice in Wonderland,* printed out by Carroll himself with his own illustrations. Complete facsimile of the "million dollar" manuscript Carroll gave to Alice Liddell in 1864. Introduction by Martin Gardner. viii + 96pp. Title and dedication pages in color. 21482-6 Paperbound **$1.50**

THE BROWNIES, THEIR BOOK, Palmer Cox. Small as mice, cunning as foxes, exuberant and full of mischief, the Brownies go to the zoo, toy shop, seashore, circus, etc., in 24 verse adventures and 266 illustrations. Long a favorite, since their first appearance in St. Nicholas Magazine. xi + 144pp. $6\frac{5}{8}$ x $9\frac{1}{4}$.
21265-3 Paperbound **$2.50**

SONGS OF CHILDHOOD, Walter De La Mare. Published (under the pseudonym Walter Ramal) when De La Mare was only 29, this charming collection has long been a favorite children's book. A facsimile of the first edition in paper, the 47 poems capture the simplicity of the nursery rhyme and the ballad, including such lyrics as I Met Eve, Tartary, The Silver Penny. vii + 106pp. (USO) 21972-0 Paperbound **$2.00**

THE COMPLETE NONSENSE OF EDWARD LEAR, Edward Lear. The finest 19th-century humorist-cartoonist in full: all nonsense limericks, zany alphabets, Owl and Pussycat, songs, nonsense botany, and more than 500 illustrations by Lear himself. Edited by Holbrook Jackson. xxix + 287pp. (USO) 20167-8 Paperbound **$3.00**

BILLY WHISKERS: THE AUTOBIOGRAPHY OF A GOAT, Frances Trego Montgomery. A favorite of children since the early 20th century, here are the escapades of that rambunctious, irresistible and mischievous goat—Billy Whiskers. Much in the spirit of *Peck's Bad Boy,* this is a book that children never tire of reading or hearing. All the original familiar illustrations by W. H. Fry are included: 6 color plates, 18 black and white drawings. 159pp. 22345-0 Paperbound **$2.75**

MOTHER GOOSE MELODIES. Faithful republication of the fabulously rare Munroe and Francis "copyright 1833" Boston edition—the most important Mother Goose collection, usually referred to as the "original." Familiar rhymes plus many rare ones, with wonderful old woodcut illustrations. Edited by E. F. Bleiler. 128pp. $4\frac{1}{2}$ x $6\frac{3}{8}$. 22577-1 Paperbound **$1.50**

HOUDINI ON MAGIC, Harold Houdini. Edited by Walter Gibson, Morris N. Young. How he escaped; exposés of fake spiritualists; instructions for eye-catching tricks; other fascinating material by and about greatest magician. 155 illustrations. 280pp. 20384-0 Pa. $2.75

HANDBOOK OF THE NUTRITIONAL CONTENTS OF FOOD, U.S. Dept. of Agriculture. Largest, most detailed source of food nutrition information ever prepared. Two mammoth tables: one measuring nutrients in 100 grams of edible portion; the other, in edible portion of 1 pound as purchased. Originally titled Composition of Foods. 190pp. 9 x 12. 21342-0 Pa. $4.00

COMPLETE GUIDE TO HOME CANNING, PRESERVING AND FREEZING, U.S. Dept. of Agriculture. Seven basic manuals with full instructions for jams and jellies; pickles and relishes; canning fruits, vegetables, meat; freezing anything. Really good recipes, exact instructions for optimal results. Save a fortune in food. 156 illustrations. 214pp. 6⅛ x 9¼. 22911-4 Pa. $2.50

THE BREAD TRAY, Louis P. De Gouy. Nearly every bread the cook could buy or make: bread sticks of Italy, fruit breads of Greece, glazed rolls of Vienna, everything from corn pone to croissants. Over 500 recipes altogether. including buns, rolls, muffins, scones, and more. 463pp. 23000-7 Pa. $3.50

CREATIVE HAMBURGER COOKERY, Louis P. De Gouy. 182 unusual recipes for casseroles, meat loaves and hamburgers that turn inexpensive ground meat into memorable main dishes: Arizona chili burgers, burger tamale pie, burger stew, burger corn loaf, burger wine loaf, and more. 120pp. 23001-5 Pa. $1.75

LONG ISLAND SEAFOOD COOKBOOK, J. George Frederick and Jean Joyce. Probably the best American seafood cookbook. Hundreds of recipes. 40 gourmet sauces, 123 recipes using oysters alone! All varieties of fish and seafood amply represented. 324pp. 22677-8 Pa. $3.50

THE EPICUREAN: A COMPLETE TREATISE OF ANALYTICAL AND PRACTICAL STUDIES IN THE CULINARY ART, Charles Ranhofer. Great modern classic. 3,500 recipes from master chef of Delmonico's, turn-of-the-century America's best restaurant. Also explained, many techniques known only to professional chefs. 775 illustrations. 1183pp. 6⅝ x 10. 22680-8 Clothbd. $22.50

THE AMERICAN WINE COOK BOOK, Ted Hatch. Over 700 recipes: old favorites livened up with wine plus many more: Czech fish soup, quince soup, sauce Perigueux, shrimp shortcake, filets Stroganoff, cordon bleu goulash, jambonneau, wine fruit cake, more. 314pp. 22796-0 Pa. $2.50

DELICIOUS VEGETARIAN COOKING, Ivan Baker. Close to 500 delicious and varied recipes: soups, main course dishes (pea, bean, lentil, cheese, vegetable, pasta, and egg dishes), savories, stews, whole-wheat breads and cakes, more. 168pp. USO 22834-7 Pa. $1.75

How to Solve Chess Problems, Kenneth S. Howard. Practical suggestions on problem solving for very beginners. 58 two-move problems, 46 3-movers, 8 4-movers for practice, plus hints. 171pp. 20748-X Pa. $2.00

A Guide to Fairy Chess, Anthony Dickins. 3-D chess, 4-D chess, chess on a cylindrical board, reflecting pieces that bounce off edges, cooperative chess, retrograde chess, maximummers, much more. Most based on work of great Dawson. Full handbook, 100 problems. 66pp. 7⅞ x 10¾. 22687-5 Pa. $2.00

Win at Backgammon, Millard Hopper. Best opening moves, running game, blocking game, back game, tables of odds, etc. Hopper makes the game clear enough for anyone to play, and win. 43 diagrams. 111pp. 22894-0 Pa. $1.50

Bidding a Bridge Hand, Terence Reese. Master player "thinks out loud" the binding of 75 hands that defy point count systems. Organized by bidding problem—no-fit situations, overbidding, underbidding, cueing your defense, etc. 254pp. EBE 22830-4 Pa. $3.00

The Precision Bidding System in Bridge, C.C. Wei, edited by Alan Truscott. Inventor of precision bidding presents average hands and hands from actual play, including games from 1969 Bermuda Bowl where system emerged. 114 exercises. 116pp. 21171-1 Pa. $1.75

Learn Magic, Henry Hay. 20 simple, easy-to-follow lessons on magic for the new magician: illusions, card tricks, silks, sleights of hand, coin manipulations, escapes, and more —all with a minimum amount of equipment. Final chapter explains the great stage illusions. 92 illustrations. 285pp. 21238-6 Pa. $2.95

The New Magician's Manual, Walter B. Gibson. Step-by-step instructions and clear illustrations guide the novice in mastering 36 tricks; much equipment supplied on 16 pages of cut-out materials. 36 additional tricks. 64 illustrations. 159pp. 6⅝ x 10. 23113-5 Pa. $3.00

Professional Magic for Amateurs, Walter B. Gibson. 50 easy, effective tricks used by professionals —cards, string, tumblers, handkerchiefs, mental magic, etc. 63 illustrations. 223pp. 23012-0 Pa. $2.50

Card Manipulations, Jean Hugard. Very rich collection of manipulations; has taught thousands of fine magicians tricks that are really workable, eye-catching. Easily followed, serious work. Over 200 illustrations. 163pp. 20539-8 Pa. $2.00

Abbott's Encyclopedia of Rope Tricks for Magicians, Stewart James. Complete reference book for amateur and professional magicians containing more than 150 tricks involving knots, penetrations, cut and restored rope, etc. 510 illustrations. Reprint of 3rd edition. 400pp. 23206-9 Pa. $3.50

The Secrets of Houdini, J.C. Cannell. Classic study of Houdini's incredible magic, exposing closely-kept professional secrets and revealing, in general terms, the whole art of stage magic. 67 illustrations. 279pp. 22913-0 Pa. $2.50

AGAINST THE GRAIN (A REBOURS), Joris K. Huysmans. Filled with weird images, evidences of a bizarre imagination, exotic experiments with hallucinatory drugs, rich tastes and smells and the diversions of its sybarite hero Duc Jean des Esseintes, this classic novel pushed 19th-century literary decadence to its limits. Full unabridged edition. Do not confuse this with abridged editions generally sold. Introduction by Havelock Ellis. xlix + 206pp.   22190-3 Paperbound **$2.50**

VARIORUM SHAKESPEARE: HAMLET. Edited by Horace H. Furness; a landmark of American scholarship. Exhaustive footnotes and appendices treat all doubtful words and phrases, as well as suggested critical emendations throughout the play's history. First volume contains editor's own text, collated with all Quartos and Folios. Second volume contains full first Quarto, translations of Shakespeare's sources (Belleforest, and Saxo Grammaticus), Der Bestrafte Brudermord, and many essays on critical and historical points of interest by major authorities of past and present. Includes details of staging and costuming over the years. By far the best edition available for serious students of Shakespeare. Total of xx + 905pp.
21004-9, 21005-7, 2 volumes, Paperbound **$11.00**

A LIFE OF WILLIAM SHAKESPEARE, Sir Sidney Lee. This is the standard life of Shakespeare, summarizing everything known about Shakespeare and his plays. Incredibly rich in material, broad in coverage, clear and judicious, it has served thousands as the best introduction to Shakespeare. 1931 edition. 9 plates. xxix + 792pp.   21967-4 Paperbound $4.50

MASTERS OF THE DRAMA, John Gassner. Most comprehensive history of the drama in print, covering every tradition from Greeks to modern Europe and America, including India, Far East, etc. Covers more than 800 dramatists, 2000 plays, with biographical material, plot summaries, theatre history, criticism, etc. "Best of its kind in English," *New Republic.* 77 illustrations. xxii + 890pp.
20100-7 Clothbound $10.00

THE EVOLUTION OF THE ENGLISH LANGUAGE, George McKnight. The growth of English, from the 14th century to the present. Unusual, non-technical account presents basic information in very interesting form: sound shifts, change in grammar and syntax, vocabulary growth, similar topics. Abundantly illustrated with quotations. Formerly *Modern English in the Making.* xii + 590pp.
21932-1 Paperbound **$4.00**

AN ETYMOLOGICAL DICTIONARY OF MODERN ENGLISH, Ernest Weekley. Fullest, richest work of its sort, by foremost British lexicographer. Detailed word histories, including many colloquial and archaic words; extensive quotations. Do not confuse this with the Concise Etymological Dictionary, which is much abridged. Total of xxvii + 830pp. 6½ x 9¼.
21873-2, 21874-0 Two volumes, Paperbound **$10.00**

FLATLAND: A ROMANCE OF MANY DIMENSIONS, E. A. Abbott. Classic of science-fiction explores ramifications of life in a two-dimensional world, and what happens when a three-dimensional being intrudes. Amusing reading, but also useful as introduction to thought about hyperspace. Introduction by Banesh Hoffmann. 16 illustrations. xx + 103pp.   20001-9 Paperbound **$1.50**

THE RED FAIRY BOOK, Andrew Lang. Lang's color fairy books have long been children's favorites. This volume includes Rapunzel, Jack and the Bean-stalk and 35 other stories, familiar and unfamiliar. 4 plates, 93 illustrations x + 367pp.
21673-X Paperbound $3.00

THE BLUE FAIRY BOOK, Andrew Lang. Lang's tales come from all countries and all times. Here are 37 tales from Grimm, the Arabian Nights, Greek Mythology, and other fascinating sources. 8 plates, 130 illustrations. xi + 390pp.
21437-0 Paperbound $3.50

HOUSEHOLD STORIES BY THE BROTHERS GRIMM. Classic English-language edition of the well-known tales — Rumpelstiltskin, Snow White, Hansel and Gretel, The Twelve Brothers, Faithful John, Rapunzel, Tom Thumb (52 stories in all). Translated into simple, straightforward English by Lucy Crane. Ornamented with headpieces, vignettes, elaborate decorative initials and a dozen full-page illustrations by Walter Crane. x + 269pp. 21080-4 Paperbound $3.00

THE MERRY ADVENTURES OF ROBIN HOOD, Howard Pyle. The finest modern versions of the traditional ballads and tales about the great English outlaw. Howard Pyle's complete prose version, with every word, every illustration of the first edition. Do not confuse this facsimile of the original (1883) with modern editions that change text or illustrations. 23 plates plus many page decorations. xxii + 296pp.
22043-5 Paperbound $4.00

THE STORY OF KING ARTHUR AND HIS KNIGHTS, Howard Pyle. The finest children's version of the life of King Arthur; brilliantly retold by Pyle, with 48 of his most imaginative illustrations. xviii + 313pp. 6⅛ x 9¼.
21445-1 Paperbound $3.50

THE WONDERFUL WIZARD OF OZ, L. Frank Baum. America's finest children's book in facsimile of first edition with all Denslow illustrations in full color. The edition a child should have. Introduction by Martin Gardner. 23 color plates, scores of drawings. iv + 267pp. 20691-2 Paperbound $3.00

THE MARVELOUS LAND OF OZ, L. Frank Baum. The second Oz book, every bit as imaginative as the Wizard. The hero is a boy named Tip, but the Scarecrow and the Tin Woodman are back, as is the Oz magic. 16 color plates, 120 drawings by John R. Neill. 287pp. 20692-0 Paperbound $3.00

THE MAGICAL MONARCH OF MO, L. Frank Baum. Remarkable adventures in a land even stranger than Oz. The best of Baum's books not in the Oz series. 15 color plates and dozens of drawings by Frank Verbeck. xviii + 237pp.
21892-9 Paperbound $2.95

THE BAD CHILD'S BOOK OF BEASTS, MORE BEASTS FOR WORSE CHILDREN, A MORAL ALPHABET, Hilaire Belloc. Three complete humor classics in one volume. Be kind to the frog, and do not call him names . . . and 28 other whimsical animals. Familiar favorites and some not so well known. Illustrated by Basil Blackwell. 156pp. (USO) 20749-8 Paperbound $2.00

VISUAL ILLUSIONS: THEIR CAUSES, CHARACTERISTICS, AND APPLICATIONS, Matthew Luckiesh. Thorough description and discussion of optical illusion, geometric and perspective, particularly; size and shape distortions, illusions of color, of motion; natural illusions; use of illusion in art and magic, industry, etc. Most useful today with op art, also for classical art. Scores of effects illustrated. Introduction by William H. Ittleson. 100 illustrations. xxi + 252pp.

21530-X Paperbound $2.50

A HANDBOOK OF ANATOMY FOR ART STUDENTS, Arthur Thomson. Thorough, virtually exhaustive coverage of skeletal structure, musculature, etc. Full text, supplemented by anatomical diagrams and drawings and by photographs of undraped figures. Unique in its comparison of male and female forms, pointing out differences of contour, texture, form. 211 figures, 40 drawings, 86 photographs. xx + 459pp. 5⅜ x 8⅜.

21163-0 Paperbound $5.00

150 MASTERPIECES OF DRAWING, Selected by Anthony Toney. Full page reproductions of drawings from the early 16th to the end of the 18th century, all beautifully reproduced: Rembrandt, Michelangelo, Dürer, Fragonard, Urs, Graf, Wouwerman, many others. First-rate browsing book, model book for artists. xviii + 150pp. 8⅜ x 11¼.

21032-4 Paperbound' $4.00

THE LATER WORK OF AUBREY BEARDSLEY, Aubrey Beardsley. Exotic, erotic, ironic masterpieces in full maturity: Comedy Ballet, Venus and Tannhauser, Pierrot, Lysistrata, Rape of the Lock, Savoy material, Ali Baba, Volpone, etc. This material revolutionized the art world, and is still powerful, fresh, brilliant. With *The Early Work,* all Beardsley's finest work. 174 plates, 2 in color. xiv + 176pp. 8⅛ x 11.

21817-1 Paperbound $4.00

DRAWINGS OF REMBRANDT, Rembrandt van Rijn. Complete reproduction of fabulously rare edition by Lippmann and Hofstede de Groot, completely reedited, updated, improved by Prof. Seymour Slive, Fogg Museum. Portraits, Biblical sketches, landscapes, Oriental types, nudes, episodes from classical mythology—All Rembrandt's fertile genius. Also selection of drawings by his pupils and followers. "Stunning volumes," *Saturday Review.* 550 illustrations. lxxviii + 552pp. 9⅛ x 12¼.

21485-0, 21486-9 Two volumes, Paperbound $12.00

THE DISASTERS OF WAR, Francisco Goya. One of the masterpieces of Western civilization—83 etchings that record Goya's shattering, bitter reaction to the Napoleonic war that swept through Spain after the insurrection of 1808 and to war in general. Reprint of the first edition, with three additional plates from Boston's Museum of Fine Arts. All plates facsimile size. Introduction by Philip Hofer, Fogg Museum. v + 97pp. 9⅜ x 8¼.

21872-4 Paperbound $3.00

GRAPHIC WORKS OF ODILON REDON. Largest collection of Redon's graphic works ever assembled: 172 lithographs, 28 etchings and engravings, 9 drawings. These include some of his most famous works. All the plates from *Odilon Redon: oeuvre graphique complet,* plus additional plates. New introduction and caption translations by Alfred Werner. 209 illustrations. xxvii + 209pp. 9⅛ x 12¼.

21966-8 Paperbound $6.00

MODERN CHESS STRATEGY, Ludek Pachman. The use of the queen, the active king, exchanges, pawn play, the center, weak squares, etc. Section on rook alone worth price of the book. Stress on the moderns. Often considered the most important book on strategy. 314pp. 20290-9 Pa. $3.50

CHESS STRATEGY, Edward Lasker. One of half-dozen great theoretical works in chess, shows principles of action above and beyond moves. Acclaimed by Capablanca, Keres, etc. 282pp. USO 20528-2 Pa. $3.00

CHESS PRAXIS, THE PRAXIS OF MY SYSTEM, Aron Nimzovich. Founder of hyper-modern chess explains his profound, influential theories that have dominated much of 20th century chess. 109 illustrative games. 369pp. 20296-8 Pa. $3.50

HOW TO PLAY THE CHESS OPENINGS, Eugene Znosko-Borovsky. Clear, profound examinations of just what each opening is intended to do and how opponent can counter. Many sample games, questions and answers. 147pp. 22795-2 Pa. $2.00

THE ART OF CHESS COMBINATION, Eugene Znosko-Borovsky. Modern explanation of principles, varieties, techniques and ideas behind them, illustrated with many examples from great players. 212pp. 20583-5 Pa. $2.50

COMBINATIONS: THE HEART OF CHESS, Irving Chernev. Step-by-step explanation of intricacies of combinative play. 356 combinations by Tarrasch, Botvinnik, Keres, Steinitz, Anderssen, Morphy, Marshall, Capablanca, others, all annotated. 245 pp. 21744-2 Pa. $3.00

HOW TO PLAY CHESS ENDINGS, Eugene Znosko-Borovsky. Thorough instruction manual by fine teacher analyzes each piece individually; many common endgame situations. Examines games by Steinitz, Alekhine, Lasker, others. Emphasis on understanding. 288pp. 21170-3 Pa. $2.75

MORPHY'S GAMES OF CHESS, Philip W. Sergeant. Romantic history, 54 games of greatest player of all time against Anderssen, Bird, Paulsen, Harrwitz; 52 games at odds; 52 blindfold; 100 consultation, informal, other games. Analyses by Anderssen, Steinitz, Morphy himself. 352pp. 20386-7 Pa. $4.00

500 MASTER GAMES OF CHESS, S. Tartakower, J. du Mont. Vast collection of great chess games from 1798-1938, with much material nowhere else readily available. Fully annotated, arranged by opening for easier study. 665pp. 23208-5 Pa. $6.00

THE SOVIET SCHOOL OF CHESS, Alexander Kotov and M. Yudovich. Authoritative work on modern Russian chess. History, conceptual background. 128 fully annotated games (most unavailable elsewhere) by Botvinnik, Keres, Smyslov, Tal, Petrosian, Spassky, more. 390pp. 20026-4 Pa. $3.95

WONDERS AND CURIOSITIES OF CHESS, Irving Chernev. A lifetime's accumulation of such wonders and curiosities as the longest won game, shortest game, chess problem with mate in 1220 moves, and much more unusual material — 356 items in all, over 160 complete games. 146 diagrams. 203pp. 23007-4 Pa. $3.50

SLEEPING BEAUTY, illustrated by Arthur Rackham. Perhaps the fullest, most delightful version ever, told by C.S. Evans. Rackham's best work. 49 illustrations. 110pp. 7⅞ x 10¾. 22756-1 Pa. $2.00

THE WONDERFUL WIZARD OF OZ, L. Frank Baum. Facsimile in full color of America's finest children's classic. Introduction by Martin Gardner. 143 illustrations by W.W. Denslow. 267pp. 20691-2 Pa. $3.00

GOOPS AND HOW TO BE THEM, Gelett Burgess. Classic tongue-in-cheek masquerading as etiquette book. 87 verses, 170 cartoons as Goops demonstrate virtues of table manners, neatness, courtesy, more. 88pp. 6½ x 9¼. 22233-0 Pa. $2.00

THE BROWNIES, THEIR BOOK, Palmer Cox. Small as mice, cunning as foxes, exuberant, mischievous, Brownies go to zoo, toy shop, seashore, circus, more. 24 verse adventures. 266 illustrations. 144pp. 6⅝ x 9¼. 21265-3 Pa. $2.50

BILLY WHISKERS: THE AUTOBIOGRAPHY OF A GOAT, Frances Trego Montgomery. Escapades of that rambunctious goat. Favorite from turn of the century America. 24 illustrations. 259pp. 22345-0 Pa. $2.75

THE ROCKET BOOK, Peter Newell. Fritz, janitor's kid, sets off rocket in basement of apartment house; an ingenious hole punched through every page traces course of rocket. 22 duotone drawings, verses. 48pp. 6⅞ x 8⅜. 22044-3 Pa. $1.50

PECK'S BAD BOY AND HIS PA, George W. Peck. Complete double-volume of great American childhood classic. Hennery's ingenious pranks against outraged pomposity of pa and the grocery man. 97 illustrations. Introduction by E.F. Bleiler. 347pp. 20497-9 Pa. $2.50

THE TALE OF PETER RABBIT, Beatrix Potter. The inimitable Peter's terrifying adventure in Mr. McGregor's garden, with all 27 wonderful, full-color Potter illustrations. 55pp. 4¼ x 5½. USO 22827-4 Pa. $1.00

THE TALE OF MRS. TIGGY-WINKLE, Beatrix Potter. Your child will love this story about a very special hedgehog and all 27 wonderful, full-color Potter illustrations. 57pp. 4¼ x 5½. USO 20546-0 Pa. $1.00

THE TALE OF BENJAMIN BUNNY, Beatrix Potter. Peter Rabbit's cousin coaxes him back into Mr. McGregor's garden for a whole new set of adventures. A favorite with children. All 27 full-color illustrations. 59pp. 4¼ x 5½. USO 21102-9 Pa. $1.00

THE MERRY ADVENTURES OF ROBIN HOOD, Howard Pyle. Facsimile of original (1883) edition, finest modern version of English outlaw's adventures. 23 illustrations by Pyle. 296pp. 6½ x 9¼. 22043-5 Pa. $4.00

TWO LITTLE SAVAGES, Ernest Thompson Seton. Adventures of two boys who lived as Indians; explaining Indian ways, woodlore, pioneer methods. 293 illustrations. 286pp. 20985-7 Pa. $3.00

150 MASTERPIECES OF DRAWING, edited by Anthony Toney. 150 plates, early 15th century to end of 18th century; Rembrandt, Michelangelo, Dürer, Fragonard, Watteau, Wouwerman, many others. 150pp. 8⅜ x 11¼.   21032-4 Pa. $4.00

THE GOLDEN AGE OF THE POSTER, Hayward and Blanche Cirker. 70 extraordinary posters in full colors, from Maîtres de l'Affiche, Mucha, Lautrec, Bradley, Cheret, Beardsley, many others. 9⅜ x 12¼.   22753-7 Pa. $4.95
21718-3 Clothbd. $7.95

SIMPLICISSIMUS, selection, translations and text by Stanley Appelbaum. 180 satirical drawings, 16 in full color, from the famous German weekly magazine in the years 1896 to 1926. 24 artists included: Grosz, Kley, Pascin, Kubin, Kollwitz, plus Heine, Thöny, Bruno Paul, others. 172pp. 8½ x 12¼.   23098-8 Pa. $5.00
23099-6 Clothbd. $10.00

THE EARLY WORK OF AUBREY BEARDSLEY, Aubrey Beardsley. 157 plates, 2 in color: Manon Lescaut, Madame Bovary, Morte d'Arthur, Salome, other. Introduction by H. Marillier. 175pp. 8½ x 11.   21816-3 Pa. $4.00

THE LATER WORK OF AUBREY BEARDSLEY, Aubrey Beardsley. Exotic masterpieces of full maturity: Venus and Tannhäuser, Lysistrata, Rape of the Lock, Volpone, Savoy material, etc. 174 plates, 2 in color. 176pp. 8½ x 11.   21817-1 Pa. $4.00

DRAWINGS OF WILLIAM BLAKE, William Blake. 92 plates from Book of Job, Divine Comedy, Paradise Lost, visionary heads, mythological figures, Laocoön, etc. Selection, introduction, commentary by Sir Geoffrey Keynes. 178pp. 8½ x 11.
22303-5 Pa. $3.50

LONDON: A PILGRIMAGE, Gustave Doré, Blanchard Jerrold. Squalor, riches, misery, beauty of mid-Victorian metropolis; 55 wonderful plates, 125 other illustrations, full social, cultural text by Jerrold. 191pp. of text. 8⅛ x 11.
22306-X Pa. $5.00

THE COMPLETE WOODCUTS OF ALBRECHT DÜRER, edited by Dr. W. Kurth. 346 in all: Old Testament, St. Jerome, Passion, Life of Virgin, Apocalypse, many others. Introduction by Campbell Dodgson. 285pp. 8½ x 12¼.   21097-9 Pa. $6.00

THE DISASTERS OF WAR, Francisco Goya. 83 etchings record horrors of Napoleonic wars in Spain and war in general. Reprint of 1st edition, plus 3 additional plates. Introduction by Philip Hofer. 97pp. 9⅜ x 8¼.   21872-4 Pa. $3.00

ENGRAVINGS OF HOGARTH, William Hogarth. 101 of Hogarth's greatest works: Rake's Progress, Harlot's Progress, Illustrations for Hudibras, Midnight Modern Conversation, Before and After, Beer Street and Gin Lane, many more. Full commentary. 256pp. 11 x 14.   22479-1 Pa. $7.00
23023-6 Clothbd. $13.50

PRIMITIVE ART, Franz Boas. Great anthropologist on ceramics, textiles, wood, stone, metal, etc.; patterns, technology, symbols, styles. All areas, but fullest on Northwest Coast Indians. 350 illustrations. 378pp.   20025-6 Pa. $3.75

EGYPTIAN MAGIC, E.A. Wallis Budge. Foremost Egyptologist, curator at British Museum, on charms, curses, amulets, doll magic, transformations, control of demons, deific appearances, feats of great magicians. Many texts cited. 19 illustrations. 234pp. USO 22681-6 Pa. $2.50

THE LEYDEN PAPYRUS: AN EGYPTIAN MAGICAL BOOK, edited by F. Ll. Griffith, Herbert Thompson. Egyptian sorcerer's manual contains scores of spells: sex magic of various sorts, occult information, evoking visions, removing evil magic, etc. Transliteration faces translation. 207pp. 22994-7 Pa. $2.50

THE MALLEUS MALEFICARUM OF KRAMER AND SPRENGER, translated, edited by Montague Summers. Full text of most important witchhunter's "Bible," used by both Catholics and Protestants. Theory of witches, manifestations, remedies, etc. Indispensable to serious student. 278pp. 6⅝ x 10. USO 22802-9 Pa. $3.95

LOST CONTINENTS, L. Sprague de Camp. Great science-fiction author, finest, fullest study: Atlantis, Lemuria, Mu, Hyperborea, etc. Lost Tribes, Irish in pre-Columbian America, root races; in history, literature, art, occultism. Necessary to everyone concerned with theme. 17 illustrations. 348pp. 22668-9 Pa. $3.50

THE COMPLETE BOOKS OF CHARLES FORT, Charles Fort. Book of the Damned, Lo!, Wild Talents, New Lands. Greatest compilation of data: celestial appearances, flying saucers, falls of frogs, strange disappearances, inexplicable data not recognized by science. Inexhaustible, painstakingly documented. Do not confuse with modern charlatanry. Introduction by Damon Knight. Total of 1126pp.
23094-5 Clothbd. $15.00

FADS AND FALLACIES IN THE NAME OF SCIENCE, Martin Gardner. Fair, witty appraisal of cranks and quacks of science: Atlantis, Lemuria, flat earth, Velikovsky, orgone energy, Bridey Murphy, medical fads, etc. 373pp. 20394-8 Pa. $3.50

HOAXES, Curtis D. MacDougall. Unbelievably rich account of great hoaxes: Locke's moon hoax, Shakespearean forgeries, Loch Ness monster, Disumbrationist school of art, dozens more; also psychology of hoaxing. 54 illustrations. 338pp. 20465-0 Pa. $3.50

THE GENTLE ART OF MAKING ENEMIES, James A.M. Whistler. Greatest wit of his day deflates Wilde, Ruskin, Swinburne; strikes back at inane critics, exhibitions. Highly readable classic of impressionist revolution by great painter. Introduction by Alfred Werner. 334pp. 21875-9 Pa. $4.00

THE BOOK OF TEA, Kakuzo Okakura. Minor classic of the Orient: entertaining, charming explanation, interpretation of traditional Japanese culture in terms of tea ceremony. Edited by E.F. Bleiler. Total of 94pp. 20070-1 Pa. $1.25

Prices subject to change without notice.
Available at your book dealer or write for free catalogue to Dept. GI, Dover Publications, Inc., 180 Varick St., N.Y., N.Y. 10014. Dover publishes more than 150 books each year on science, elementary and advanced mathematics, biology, music, art, literary history, social sciences and other areas.